EASTWARD HO!
THE FIRST ENGLISH ADVENTURERS TO THE ORIENT

CZAR IVAN VASSILIVITCH

*From woodcut in "Early Voyages and
Travels to Russia & Persia," Hakluyt
Society, Volumes 72 and 73, 1886*

EASTWARD HO!

THE FIRST ENGLISH ADVENTURERS TO THE ORIENT—RICHARD CHANCELLOR—ANTHONY JENKINSON—JAMES LANCASTER—WILLIAM ADAMS—SIR THOMAS ROE

By

FOSTER RHEA DULLES

WITH TWENTY ILLUSTRATIONS

Essay Index Reprint Series

BOOKS FOR LIBRARIES PRESS
FREEPORT, NEW YORK

First Published 1931
Reprinted 1969

G
245
D8
1969

STANDARD BOOK NUMBER:
8369-1256-X

LIBRARY OF CONGRESS CATALOG CARD NUMBER:
73-90632

PRINTED IN THE UNITED STATES OF AMERICA

TO MARTY

Sail forth! steer for deep waters only!
Reckless, O soul, exploring, I with thee, and thou with me
For we are bound where mariner has not yet dared to go,
And we will risk the ship, ourselves and all.

WALT WHITMAN.

PREFACE

ANY reference to English voyages in the age of Elizabeth invokes a picture of the reckless raids of Drake and Hawkins, the depredations of the buccaneers of the Spanish Main, or the voyages of discovery along the northern coast of America by such men as Frobisher and Davis. The pioneers in England's discovery of the East who found their way about the North Cape in the search for Cathay, who penetrated to Persia and Central Asia, who eventually sought out India, the Spice Islands and Japan, stand almost neglected. Yet they were men who were no less daring and adventurous than these other seamen of Elizabeth, and their service to England was no less important. They laid the foundation for English trade in the East and all unknowing pointed the way to Empire.

F. R. D.

New York, 1930

CONTENTS

PAGE

PREFACE ix

I. RICHARD CHANCELLOR

CHAPTER
I. THE SAILING OF THE "EDWARD BONAVENTURE"   1
II. THE NORTH-EAST FROSTIE SEA 5
III. THE COURT OF IVAN THE TERRIBLE . . . 13
IV. TRADE WITH MUSCOVY 26

II. ANTHONY JENKINSON

V. THE ROAD TO BOKHARA 39
VI. THE GREAT SOPHIE 54
VII. ENVOY OF ELIZABETH 63

III. JAMES LANCASTER

VIII. A CHALLENGE TO PORTUGAL 77
IX. THE RICH AND GOULDEN ISLAND 89
X. JAVA AND THE PASSAGE HOME . . . 104

IV. WILLIAM ADAMS

XI. THE WESTWARD VOYAGE 113
XII. COUNCILLOR OF IYEYASU 121
XIII. THE ENGLISH FACTORY 135

V. SIR THOMAS ROE

XIV. A ROYAL AMBASSADOR 153
XV. THE GREAT MOGUL 162
XVI. SPLENDOUR AND INTRIGUE 174
NOTES 187
SOURCES 191
INDEX 195

xi

LIST OF ILLUSTRATIONS

CZAR IVAN VASSILIVITCH . . . . . . *Frontispiece*
From *woodcut in "Early Voyages and Travels to Russia and Persia," Hakluyt Society, volumes 72 and 73, 1886*

SEA WONDERS OF THE UNKNOWN NORTH . . . *Facing page* 8
From *Sebastian Munster's " Comographia (1544), 1628 "*

THE KREMLIN . . . . " " 32
From *"Voyages de Corneille le Brun par la Moscovie en Perse et aux Indes Orientales, 1718 "*

JENKINSON'S MAP OF RUSSIA . . . . *Between pages* 40-41
From *Ortelius' "Theatrum Orbis Terrarum "*

SPORT AT AN EASTERN CAPITAL . . . . . *Facing page* 50
From *Thevenot's "Voyages," 1727*

JUSTICE AT THE PERSIAN COURT . . . . . " " 58
From *Thevenot's "Voyages "*

PLAN OF MOSCOW . . . . " " 70
From *Sigismund von Herberstein's "Rerum Moscoviticarum Commentarii," 1549*

SIXTEENTH CENTURY MAP SHOWING NORTH-EAST AND NORTH-WEST PASSAGES . . . . *Between pages* 78-79
From *Theatram Orbis Terrarum of Abraham Ortelius, 1573*

THE HARBOUR OF MALACCA . . . . . . *Facing page* 82
From *Constantin de Renneville's "Recuei des Voyages," 1725*

A ROYAL ELEPHANT . . . . " " 92
From *Churchill's "Voyages," 1744*

NAVAL WARFARE IN THE INDIES . . . . . " " 100
From *Churchill's "Voyages "*

STORM AT SEA . . . . " " 106
From *Johan Nieuhof's "Die Gesantschaft der Ost-Indischen Geselschaft in den Vereinigten Niederlanden," 1666*

FRONTISPIECE AND TITLE PAGE OF " PURCHAS HIS PILGRIMES "
From *Edition of 1625* *Between pages* 114-115

INLAND SEA . . . . *Facing page* 122
From *Arnoldus Montanus' "Ambassades memorables . . vers les Empereurs du Japon," 1680*

THE COURT OF THE SHOGAN . . . . . *Facing page* 130
From Montanus' "Ambassades memorables"

YEDO . . . . „ „ 140
From Montanus' "Ambassades memorables"

SIR THOMAS ROE . . . . „ „ 160
From the portrait by M. J. Van Miereveldt in the National Gallery, by permission of Emery Walker Ltd.

A DURBAR . . . . „ „ 166
From "Voyages de François Bernier," contenant description des États du Grand Mogul, 1699

THE BIRTHDAY CEREMONY . . . . . . „ „ 172
From "Voyages de François Bernier"

THE GREAT MOGUL ON THE MARCH . . . „ „ 180
From "Voyages de François Bernier"

I

RICHARD CHANCELLOR, *died* 1556.

"A man of great estimation for many good partes of wit in him."

CLEMENT ADAMS, 1577.

CHAPTER I

THE SAILING OF
THE "EDWARD BONAVENTURE"

ON the 10th of May, 1553, some few weeks before
the death of " our most dread Soveraigne Lord,
and King, Edward the Sixt," a fleet of three
ships weighed anchor at Ratcliffe on the Thames and
slowly dropped down stream with the ebb tide. There
was something strangely moving in the farewells the
seamen paid to those friends and kinsfolk who had come
to see them off. For this was no ordinary voyage to the
coast of Holland or France on which the fleet was
setting forth. Its goal was nothing less than the discovery of Cathay and " divers other regions, dominions,
Islands, and places unknowen " which might lie beyond
the uncharted seas to the north-east. [1]

Five more years were to pass before Elizabeth came to
the English throne, but the spirit of daring and of
adventurous vitality behind this voyage in 1553 was that
which later characterized her reign and sent forth Drake
and Cavendish, Frobisher and John Davis. England
was already awakening. She was reaching out into
the unknown. Her seamen were ready to dare every
danger to search out the legendary land which Columbus
was seeking when he happened upon the New World.
No risk could turn them aside from their hunt for
those remote regions which the glowing accounts
of Marco Polo had first taught the West to believe
were " replenished with infynyt Treasures, as golde,

sylver, precious stones, baumes, spices, drogges and gummes."

Sir Hugh Willoughby, a valiant gentleman who had fought in the Scottish campaigns of Henry VIII, headed this first expedition to the north-east. His second-in-command and the pilot-major of his fleet was Richard Chancellor, chosen for this post from among many applicants because in him alone " great hope for the performance of the business rested." A protégé of Henry Sidney—the father of Sir Philip—Chancellor had had some experience as a seaman. He had sailed with Roger Bodenham on his exciting venture into the territories of the Great Turk. But beyond this meagre fact we know nothing of him at this time except that he was a widower, whose two sons he feared might be left orphans as a result of the venturesome voyage which he was undertaking.

The three vessels for which he was pilot-major were called " great ships " in the sixteenth century. To-day we could put them all on the decks of an ocean liner. The " Bona Esperanza," " admiral " of the fleet, was 120 tons burden ; the " Edward Bonaventure," Chancellor's ship, 160 ; and the " Bona Confidentia," 90. The crews and passengers totalled 118. Fifty of these men were on the " Edward Bonaventure," whose master—for Chancellor as pilot-major did not have a direct command—was Stephen Burroughs, and whose mate was John Buckland. The ship's roster shows that there were on board her two merchants, seven gentlemen adventurers, a minister and a surgeon. In the crew itself were a master gunner and his mate, two gunners, a boatswain and mate, four quartermasters, a steward and his mate, a cook, a cooper, a carpenter and twenty-one seamen. Like the other two boats, the " Edward Bonaventure " carried a cargo of English woollens, had a pinnace and a small boat stowed away in her waist, was

armed with " al manner of artillerie," and furnished with
eighteen months' provision of the sour beer, hard biscuit,
salt pork and cheese which in that day made up the most
part of a seaman's diet. [2]

They were clumsy little vessels with their short masts,
their high poops and forecastles. They answered
awkwardly to the helm and pitched dangerously in a
high sea. The crowded, dark and noisome cabins
beneath their decks were pestilential holes for the seamen
forced to live in them for months on end. Yet ships
even smaller had brought Columbus across the Atlantic
in his search for Cathay and Cipangu. Ships of the same
tonnage were during the next half-century to open
England's trade with the East and lay the foundations
for England's empire. It was the men in them who
counted.

As the anchors then were weighed on the " Good
Hope," the " Good Adventure," and the " Good Confidence "—symbolic names for voyages on unknown
seas !—the fleet sailed easily down the Thames, the
gleaming white sails billowing in the wind, the high,
carved prows breasting the water ; the sailors, in their
special holiday attire of sky blue, made a brave sight for
the people who flocked to the river bank to see them pass.
The mariners called and hallooed to their friends on
shore, and for their final farewells scrambled into the
shrouds or climbed to the tops of the masts. They
shouted " in such sort, that the skie rang againe with the
noyse thereof."

As the three ships came near Greenwich, where King
Edward was then staying, the courtiers mingled with
the throngs gathered on the bank of the Thames. The
press on shore grew thicker and thicker, the excitement
on the river ran even higher. But Edward himself,
in whose honour the ships were flying all their flags
and pennants, lay ill. He could not see the departure

of the expedition on which England was setting such hopes and to whose leaders he had entrusted letters sweepingly addressed to " all Kings, Princes, Rulers, Judges, and Governours of the earth, and all other having any excellent dignitie on the same, in all places under the universall heaven." King Edward lay dying, little realizing that a new era of English voyages and discoveries was being ushered in with the booming of the ships' guns which he could hear echoing over the hills, and then faintly reflected in the shouts of the sailors.

There were officers of his realm to bid the seamen God-speed, however. " The privie Counsel," wrote the chronicler of the voyage of the " Edward Bonaventure," " they lookt out at the windowes of the Court, and the rest ranne up to the toppes of the towers." Again the guns boomed as the " shippes shoot off their pieces after the manner of warre " ; again the shouts of the sailors in the rigging rent the air.

So the fleet passed Greenwich. Still going down slowly with the tide, sometimes under sail and sometimes towed by the ships' small boats, the three vessels reached the river's mouth and then sailed on to Harwich. There they waited for a favourable wind. After a long delay, which caused anxiety because some of the supplies were already becoming putrefied and several hogsheads of wine had been found to be leaky, they finally got under way. The season was too far advanced to wait for additional provisions. Sails were hoisted, and with final backward glances at the receding shores of England the seamen " committed themselves to the sea, giving their last adieu to their native Countrey, which they knewe not whether they should ever returne to see againe or not."

CHAPTER II

THE NORTH-EAST FROSTIE SEA

IT was not only among the common people along the Thames or among the courtiers of Edward VI that the sailing of these three ships for Cathay evoked such great excitement. The merchants of London were even more deeply interested. It was they who had despatched the fleet to the East, and it was freighted with their hopes for new trade. Romance and adventure have cast their glamour over the voyages of the sixteenth century, but they did not launch the ships. It was trade.

Yet, after all, what human activity has more possible romance than trade? Since caravans first passed over the deserts of Mesopotamia with " their camels bearing spicery, and balm, and myrrh," or the ships of Solomon sailed from Ophir

> " With a cargo of ivory
> And apes and peacocks,
> Sandalwood, cedarwood, and sweet white wine,"

commerce has strangely stirred man's imagination. London's merchants could not escape its spell. The Indies were the pot of gold at the rainbow's end and every breeze from the East was fragrant with spices.

The genesis of the voyage undertaken by Willoughby and Chancellor is explained to us by Clement Adams in more prosaic terms. He speaks of the loss of markets for English wool and of a new demand for imported luxuries with " forreine Marchandise in great accompt,

5

and their prices wonderfully raised." "Certaine grave Citizens of London" pondered over this problem and "it was at last concluded that three shippes should be prepared and furnished out, for the search and discoverie of the Northerne part of the world, to open a way and passage to our men for travaile to newe and unknowen kingdomes."

When we seek somewhat further for the motives behind this voyage, and for the reason why it set out towards the north-east, we find a ready explanation in the activities of Spain and Portugal. Drawn by that trade which had been partially shut off from the West by Moslem domination of the land routes of Central Asia, Columbus had sailed westward and Vasco da Gama had followed Diaz round the Cape of Good Hope. From the one voyage had grown Spain's wealth in the West Indies, from the other Portugal's Empire in the East. Together the two nations had discovered the unknown world, and the Pope nonchalantly divided it between them. England was completely excluded.

For one brief moment the merchants of London had thought they might win some part of this new-found wealth through the discoveries of John Cabot. He had returned from his explorations along the northern coast of the New World confident that he had found Cathay, and that somewhere near at hand lay Cipangu, where all the world's precious stones and spices were believed to have their origin. He called himself Lord Admiral, dressed in silks and gave an island to his barber. But England was soon disillusioned. North America was not Cathay. It was a vast obstruction lying athwart all England's hopes, and a score of explorers were vainly to seek a passage through it to the lands which lay so far beyond.

As early as 1527, however, the idea that if Cathay could not be reached by the west it might be sought by the north and east was first broached by Robert Thorne, an English merchant in Seville. He saw the need of England to bestir herself when " out of Spaine they have discovered all the Indies and Seas Occidentall, and out of Portingall all the Indies and Seas Orientall." And he was positive the northern seas were navigable. This stout Briton would not admit that there was land or sea through which his countrymen could not make their way. He believed that the perpetual light of the Arctic summers would make the task of finding a northern passage to the East far simpler than that which had faced the Portuguese and Spanish in the south.

His plan was an ingenious one. It was to sail directly across the North Pole, for somehow he had become convinced that the bitter cold of the north became more temperate the nearer one approached what another scornful geographer called " a Point, but Nothing, but Vanitie." Once the English ships reached the Pole, he told Henry VIII, " it is plaine they may decline to what part they list." They could sail through temperate seas to " Cathaio Oriental, which is of all the maine land most Orientall," to Tartary, to the " land of Chinas," to the Moluccas, the Indies and " the backe side of the new found land "; they could sail directly south to the tropics where they would find " the richest landes and Islands of the world." (3)

There was no one in his day to point out the impossibility of navigating the frozen seas of the Arctic Circle. No one had penetrated their icy waters. And even after expedition after expedition had returned from fruitless attempts to do so the belief was common among geographers for almost a hundred years that somewhere in the north lay a warm and open passage to the fabled East. Richard Hakluyt, to whose unflagging interest in English voyages we owe almost all we know of these early attempts to find Cathay, was convinced of it. He

confidently asked Arthur Pet and Charles Jackman to
bring home a young man from Cambaluc when they
sailed off to the north-east in 1580. Gerardus Mercator
wrote in the same year that " the voyage to Cathaio by
the East, is doubtlesse very easie and short."

Anthony Jenkinson, whose own travels on the road to
Cathay we shall have occasion to follow, advanced what
he considered undoubted proof of the illusive passage in
a petition to Queen Elizabeth. Like Thorne, he was
obsessed by the idea that, with three of the four parts of
the world already discovered, it was for England to find
the " famous Region of Cathaye and Infynyte Ilondes
neare thereunto " where the merchants of London could
sell their wool and find spices, jewels and gold " in greate
habondanns."

Jenkinson had heard of the discovery of a unicorn's
horn—a more scientific age would probably have recognized it as the tusk of a narwhal—off the Russian coast.
Knowing that " Unycornes are Bredde in the Landes of
Cathaye, Chynaye and other Orientall Regions," it was
an easy step to demonstrate that the horn could only
have been brought to Russia by the tides flooding
through a channel from the Sea of Chin. This thesis did
not go unanswered even in the sixteenth century, however. Jenkinson found a sceptical opponent to his
views in no less an authority than Sir Humphrey Gilbert.
" First it is doubtful whether these barbarous Tartarians
do know an Unicornes horne, when they see it, yea or
no," this rationalist told Queen Elizabeth, " and if it
were one, yet it is not credible that the sea could have
driven it so farre, being of such nature that it will not
swimme."

With such arguments were the possibilities of a North-
east Passage debated in England from the days of Robert
Thorne to those of Henry Hudson. Is it any wonder
that in the middle of this period, when the ice-strewn

SEA WONDERS OF THE UNKNOWN NORTH

From Sebastian Munster's
"Cosmographia" (1544), 1628

waters of the northern seas were still entirely uncharted, the merchants of London sent off their ships to discover Cathay by this route rather than by the better-known but equally illusive passage to the north-west?

Furthermore, this venture we have seen setting out from London in 1553 had the backing of Sebastian Cabot —" a man in those days very renowmed." In fact this shrewd pilot, whose own exploits have become inextricable confused with those of his father, enjoyed a startling reputation for geographical knowledge. He had returned to England in 1548 from his service with the King of Spain and had almost immediately become the moving spirit in the formation of the " Marchants Adventurers of England, for the discovery of lands, territories, Iles, Dominions, and Seignories unknowen." When he suggested they should send out a voyage to the north-east, it was natural that his advice should be followed.

The new company had been unable to find out any definite information of the land towards which their ships were heading. By some chance there were two Tartary stableboys in the employ of King Edward, but when the merchants sent for them it was soon discovered that they were too dense and stupid to be able to give any clear account of their country. The sole reliance of the voyagers was upon the geographical theories of Cabot. With a charter from the King and £6,000 capital they unhesitatingly went ahead with their plans to push back the frontiers of the unknown world for the sake of English trade.

We have seen that Sir Hugh Willoughby headed the expedition and that Richard Chancellor was second-in-command. The former had been chosen because he had had experience in leading men and because of " his goodly personage (for he was of a tall stature) "; the latter because he had some knowledge of navigation and had been urged upon the company by Henry Sidney.

" I doe now part with Chancelor," Sidney told the merchant adventurers, " not because I make little reckoning of the man, or that his maintenance is burdensome and chargeable unto mee, but that you might conceive and understand my good will and promptitude for the furtherance of this businesse, and that the authoritie and estimation which hee deserveth may be given him. You know the man by report, I by experience, you by wordes, I by deedes, you by speech and companie, and I by the daily triall of his life have a full and perfect knowledge of him."

After this eulogy, wrote Clement Adams, those among the company who knew Chancellor began " to conceive a speciall hope, that the man would prove in time very rare and excellent, and that his vertues already appearing and shining to the world would growe to the great honour and advancement of this kingdome."

Despite the merchants' faith in the leaders of their expedition, it is only too easy to see that, whatever their moral qualities might be, they were not especially strong on practical experience. Here again reliance had been placed upon Sebastian Cabot, who provided the voyagers with detailed instructions. They are not only a valuable and picturesque commentary on this voyage ; they may be taken as the model for the instructions given all later ventures of this kind, including those sent out in the next century by the great East India Company.

In the first place Cabot enjoined the seamen to observe " unitie, love, conformitie and obedience " and to endeavour by every means possible to keep together " and not separate themselves asunder." The second rule was one to which every explorer who followed in their trail was deeply indebted : " Item, that the marchants, and other skilful persons in writing, shal daily write, describe, and put in memorie the Navigation of every day and night, with the points, and observation of the lands, tides, elements, altitude of the sunne, course of the moon and starres."

Further on the long list we find two " items " which both illustrate the religious turmoil through which England was then passing, and the pious spirit which characterized the age. The seamen were " not to disclose to any nation the state of our religion, but to passe it over in silence," yet they were to observe all the forms of their Protestant faith while on shipboard. Morning and evening prayers were to be read daily, no blaspheming, swearing or ungodly talk was to be tolerated, and " neither dicing, carding, tabling, nor other divelish games to be frequented." A deeply religious atmosphere was to become typical of all voyages of trade, discovery or open piracy throughout the approaching Elizabethan period. However the acts of English sailors might at times seem to belie the dictates of Christianity, they put their trust in God and, as Cabot advised, piously observed all the forms of prayer and worship.

The instructions for the attitude to be shown towards whatever natives the expedition might come across are significant of another characteristic of the English voyages which serves to distinguish them from the voyages of Spain and Portugal. England sought new lands neither to conquer them nor to proselytize them. At this period her sole aim was trade and the peaceful acquisition of new markets. Her attitude towards the peoples of the East was both friendly and conciliatory. Consequently the seamen on this voyage were warned not to provoke the natives " by any disdaine, laughing, contempt, or such like," however much their customs might differ from those of Englishmen.

But at the same time Cabot was practical. He advised the voyagers to go ashore only in strength and to

keep near their ships.   Question the natives in a kindly
way about their countries, he ordered, and then shrewdly
added, " If the person taken may be made drunke with
your beere, or wine, you shal know the secrets of his
heart."

Perhaps this last bit of guile had been suggested by
his own experiences on the coast of America.   Certainly
one other warning seems to be born of personal observation : " If you shall see them weare Lyons or Beares
skinnes, having long bowes, and arrowes, be not afraid
of that sight : for such be worne oftentimes more to
feare strangers, then for any other cause."

And finally this master strategist for the discovery of
unknown kingdoms wrote :   " Item no conspiracies,
parttakings, factions, false tales, untrue reports . . . with
daily remembrances of the great importance of the
voyage, the honour, glorie, praise, and benefite that
depend of, and upon the same, toward the common
wealth of this noble Realme, the advancement of you
the travailers therein, your wives and children . . .
praying the living God, to give you his grace, to accom-
plish your charge to his glorie, whose merciful hand shal
prosper your voyage, and preserve you from all dangers."

This was our seamen's benediction.   And as they
sailed the merchant adventurers in London sat back in
confident expectation that in good time the three ships
would return with their cargoes of wool exchanged at
great profit for the riches of the East.   Spain and
Portugal were to be circumvented and England was to
become mistress of a safe and easy passage to Cathay
through the " north-east frostie sea."

CHAPTER III

THE COURT OF IVAN THE TERRIBLE

SAILING north-east from Harwich the three ships made their way along the East Anglian coast and, when on June 23 they finally cleared Orford Ness, struck off due north. It was a slow voyage, " traversing and tracing the seas, by reason of sundry and manifold contrary windes," but in due time they reached the coast of Norway and the island of Senjen. There they sought to find a pilot to take them round the North Cape to the Danish stronghold of Vardo, the outpost of European civilization in the north-east beyond which no English ship had ever sailed except for a mythical voyage in the days of King Alfred.

A sudden storm now caused the collapse of their plans. The little fleet were precipitately blown out to sea, and that night " by violence of winde, and thicke-nesse of mists, we were not able to keepe within sight." The first rule of Sebastian Cabot was violated, through no fault of the seamen, and it was a dire portent. The " Edward Bonaventure " never again sighted either the " Bona Esperanza " or the " Bona Confidentia."

The seas about the North Cape can be stormy and tempestuous ; on this fateful night they were " out-ragious." Chancellor's tiny ship was tossed about mercilessly and only by the most skilful seamanship was he able to keep it on its course and eventually make Vardo. Here the " Edward Bonaventure " waited a week for its companion vessels, but when they failed to reach the appointed rendezvous the expedition which had started out so bravely seemed to be doomed. Chancellor, we read, became " very pensive, heavie, and sorrowfull."

This was his first test, and in the way he met it we gain some insight into his character. Ignorant of the fate of the other vessels, and fearing the worst, he nevertheless decided to sail on into the unknown with his single ship. There were certain Scotchmen at Vardo who endeavoured to dissuade him and painted fearful pictures of the terrors of the Arctic seas. Their warnings only strengthened his determination.

It is Clement Adams who tells us how these men urged him to turn back, " but hee holding nothing so ignominious and reprochfull, as inconstancie and levitie of minde, and perswading himselfe that a man of valour coulde not commit a more dishonourable part then for feare of danger to avoyde and shunne great attempts, was nothing at all changed or discouraged with the speeches and words of the Scots, remaining stedfast and immutable in his first resolution : determining either to bring that to passe which was intended, or els to die the death."

And even more remarkable than his own valour was the willingness of his crew to follow him. Often in the narratives of the voyages of this day we read of seamen refusing to sail their ship on the course plotted by the master. Again and again they forced their leaders to turn back. In this instance, despite serious " cogitations and perturbations of minde," they were with Chancellor to the man. He was not only brave himself, he inspired bravery and loyalty in others. These two qualities saved the first venture to the north-east from complete failure.

When, finally, hope for the " Bona Confidentia " and

the " Bona Esperanza " had been given up, Chancellor set out eastward and came " at last to the place hee found no night at all, but a continuall light and brightnesse of the Sunne shining clearely upon the huge and mightie Sea." It was August. The English sailors were experiencing that perpetual daylight of the Arctic summer which Robert Thorne had thought would be such an aid to the discovery of a passage to Cathay.

They now turned south and after some days came upon a narrow opening into a great bay. Was this the passage to the East ? Probably Chancellor and his men thought so. Certainly they had no idea where they were. They had discovered something, and with high hopes prepared to find out what it was. But the bleak coastline which opened up before them gave little promise of turning out to be the Cathay of which they had heard such fabulous tales.

Before long they came upon a small boat filled with native fishermen. It fled before them, and when finally overtaken its crew grovelled in abject fear before the tall strangers and their great ship. But Chancellor had not read Cabot's instructions in vain. " Hee (according to his great and singular courtesie,) looked pleasantly upon them, comforting them by signs and gestures." He raised them up " in all loving sort." Then to his astonishment the English pilot learned that he was in the territory of the " barbarous Russe," the kingdom of the Duke of Muscovy. He had thought to discover Cathay and had found Russia. The passage which he had hoped would lead him into the Sea of Chin had led to the White Sea.

England, of course, knew of Russia in this period, but there is no evidence in the documents concerning this voyage that the merchants of London had any idea that the ships they had despatched to the north-east would touch its shores. (4) Their geographical conception of

the great northern empire was far too hazy. All that
was known of Russia had been learned through the
reports of foreign travellers who had made their way to
Moscow overland. There is no record of any Englishman ever having visited the country, though it is of
course possible that stray wanderers may have crossed
the Polish or Lithuanian frontier. Chancellor was
certainly the first of his countrymen to approach the
Czar's empire by way of the northern seas. Probably
he was the first Englishman who was ever in Russia
at all.

If his decision at Vardo had been the turning-point of
his expedition, the choice he now made ensured its
success. With Cathay how many miles further east he
did not know and the season already turning cold, he
decided to seek trade in Russia. It might not produce
the gold and silver, the silks and spices, he had hoped to
find, but it did seem to offer a perfect market for English
woollens. The goal of his voyage was Cathay only
because it meant trade. Here was possible trade nearer
home of which London had not dreamed.

Chancellor went ashore on August 24, more than
three months after sailing from London, landing at
the small village of Nenoksa. It was on the River
Dvina, near the site of the modern Archangel. The
English were cordially received by the people and local
officials of Nenoksa, yet such was the autocratic control
of the Russian Czar, Ivan Vassilivitch, Duke of Muscovy,
that his subjects dared not trade with the new-comers
without his special permission. Chancellor proposed
that he should proceed overland to Moscow to seek this
permission himself, but even before this was done the
Russians felt it necessary to send off messengers to the
Czar to discover if this was his will.

Such servility was new to the Englishman. He
refused to await the Czar's permission. As an envoy of

King Edward, armed with his precious letter to all the
rulers of the world, he had no intention of allowing his
plans to be stayed by local Russian officials. His
authority overruled their objections, and somewhat
reluctantly they provided him with the sleds and horses
which early winter made necessary for the long trip to
Court. Leaving the " Edward Bonaventure " and most
of the crew in safe quarters at Unskaia Bay, Chancellor
set out for Moscow.

As the little party sped over the snow-packed roads
which crossed the northern plains, they found the cold
" very extreme and horrible." It was like nothing the
Englishmen had ever experienced before. By day they
seemed to drive on endlessly, muffled in furs and woollens, over a countryside drear and desolate ; by night
they huddled about the stove in some villager's flat-
roofed wooden cabin. When only a few days on their
journey, however, they were encouraged by the return
of the messengers the officials of Nenoksa had sent on
ahead. The Czar was enthusiastic over the unexpected
arrival of English traders. He welcomed them with
exaggerated cordiality and sent specific instructions to his
officials to speed them on their way to Moscow with all
honour. The effect of these orders was magical. The
attitude of the people with whom the English came in
contact changed overnight from grudging compliance
with their requests for food and shelter, to vigorous
rivalry to serve them in every way. At every village the
Russians " began to quarrel, yea, and to fight also in
striving and contending which of them should put their
post horses to the sledde."

We do not know how long the fifteen-hundred-mile
trip to Moscow took the travellers or just when they
reached the capital. All we can discover is that it was
a " very long and troublesome journey." When they
at last did arrive it was to find a city " greater than

2

London with the suburbes," a straggling conglomera-
tion of wooden houses with innumerable churches and
monasteries.   Chancellor wrote that it was " very rude "
and " standeth without all order."   Even the Kremlin
with its brick walls and surrounding moat was " not of
the neatest."   It did not compare with the palaces which
the Englishman had seen in both his own country and
in France.

Russia was, in fact, but half-civilized in the middle of
the sixteenth century.   Its people hovered on the
borderland of barbarism much as their Czar, who came
to be called Ivan the Terrible, hovered on the edge of
insanity.   They were a hard and rude people.   They
kept their wives in close subjection and did not spare the
whip.   They delighted " in eating of grosse meates and
stinking fishes."   They loved their wine with an abiding
passion.   They were quarrelsome and violent, fierce
riders and brave fighters.

Some ten years after Chancellor's visit another Englishman, George Turberville, gave a rhyming account of the
Muscovites as he had found them :

> " A people passing rude, to vices vile inclinde,
>   Folke fit to be of Bacchus traine, so quaffing is their kinde
>   Drinke is their whole desire, the pot is all their pride,
>   The sobrest head doth once a day stand needfull of a guide."

To Chancellor there was something admirable in at
least one phase of their rudeness.   Writing to his uncle,
one Christopher Frothingham, in a letter which he titled
"The booke of the great and mighty Emperor of Russia,"
he described the life of the soldiers, who subsisted
on so little food that it was hard to see how they kept
alive and slept at night on the frozen ground without
cover.   "There be no such people under the sunne
for their hardnesse of living," he declared admiringly.

He wished the soldiers of England could bear such hardships and would serve as obediently as these iron-ruled
serfs of the Russian Czar. " Oh that our own sturdie
rebels were had in the like subjection to knowe their
duety towarde their Princes."

The English had immediately recognized the autocratic authority of a ruler who caused all matters to
" passe his judgement be they ever so small." At this
time Ivan was at the height of his glory. He had just
returned from the conquest of Kazan and assumed his
title of Czar. He had confessed the sins of his lurid boy-
hood and surrounded himself with able councillors. He
was both feared and loved.

Yet the days when his fits of ungovernable fury were to
sweep everything before them, when his cruel madness
was to earn him the name of Ivan the Terrible, were not
far off. Then he was to throw those courtiers who
offended him to his dogs, kill his own son in a wild
outbreak of rage, and ravage the countryside with those
fierce bands of " oprichniki " whose insignia was a dog's
head and a broom, but who wore the frocks of monks
when they returned from their raids to carouse with
their master in the Kremlin. Then he was to cause
thousands of the innocent citizens of Novgorod to be
driven to their death in a hole cut through the ice on the
Volga. In the rude and vicious society of sixteenth-
century Russia, Ivan the Terrible was to become rude
and vicious far beyond those who surrounded him.

Chancellor and his companions could not know of
this. They found a monarch friendly and cordial,
whose welcome proved that he had the vision to appreciate the advantages of this new contact with western
Europe. He was deeply interested in trade. Within a
few days of their arrival the English were requested to
send their leaders to an audience at Court.

Chancellor and two of his companions went to the

Kremlin. They first entered a large room where a hundred courtiers sat in state, gowned in robes of cloth of gold which fell to their ankles. Conducted through this chamber to an inner hall they were ushered into the presence of the Czar himself. Surrounded by his favourite councillors he was upon his throne, his crown of burnished gold, his robe " all of Goldsmiths worke," and a " staffe of Cristall and golde in his right hand." There was " a Majestie in his countenance proportionable with the excellencie of his estate."

The English were deeply impressed with the pomp and grandeur of this scene. Clement Adams declared it almost " dasht them out of confidence." But Chancellor rose to the occasion with dignity and diplomatic address. " Nothing dismaied," he stepped gravely forward, saluted the Czar in the manner of Englishmen addressing their sovereign, and handed him the royal letter from King Edward. As a contemporary poet wrote : [5]

> " Let passe what paste in speech betwixt
> Our pilot and their king :
> Full well could Chancelor demeane
> Himselfe in every thing."

The visitors were dismissed after a few questions but summoned to appear again in two hours for a royal banquet. The scene which greeted them upon their return was one of even more barbaric splendour than that of their first audience. Everything seemed to be made of gold. In the centre of the banqueting-hall was a huge cupboard loaded with the Czar's own gold plate— " very massie." About the sides of the room were set tables with benches for a hundred guests, so laden with gold vessels " that there was no roome for some to stand upon them." The richness of the courtiers' robes beggared description, and even the hundred and forty servitors wore a livery of cloth of gold.

" What shall I further say ? " asked Chancellor in describing a display of wealth which the King of England could not hope to equal. " I never heard nor saw men so sumptuous."

The banqueting itself was a ceremonious affair. Before the first course was served the Czar sent a piece of bread to each guest in turn. One hundred times it was loudly announced : " The Great Duke of Moscovie, and chiefe Emperor of Russia, John Basiliwich (& then the officer nameth the guest) doth give thee bread." When he himself was served the Czar crossed himself and the whole company rose.

Long before the interminable succession of courses, which began with roast swan, had been served, candles had to be brought in. Then when the final dish had been cleared away the Czar called his nobles before him one by one and dismissed them for the night. " It is a wonder," Chancellor observed, " to heare howe he could name them, having so many as he hath." But this was the subtle method whereby Ivan succeeded in keeping himself accurately informed of just what went on in his Court.

Chancellor and his men spent the whole winter at Moscow. They could not have returned over the frozen northern seas in any event, but as a matter of fact the cordiality of the Czar continued to reflect the graciousness he had shown them on their arrival. Certain Flemish traders at Novgorod, jealous for the trading monopoly they had maintained until the arrival of the English, endeavoured to convince Ivan that the newcomers were " pirats and rovers." He paid no attention to these tales but gave the English every opportunity to trade and perfect freedom of action.

During this period Chancellor proved that he had exceptional diplomatic skill. The tone he adopted in his dealings with the proud Czar of all the Russias was

nicely calculated to win favour and at the same time
uphold the dignity of his own position as England's first
representative at the Court of Muscovy. He encouraged
Ivan to hope for closer relations with England and
pointed out the advantages which would accrue to both
countries from the new commerce.

So successful were his representations that before he
was ready to leave he had obtained the Czar's formal
assent to a continuation of the trade which had been
inaugurated. As events were to prove, Ivan had hopes
of this commercial intercourse leading to closer ties
between England and Russia, but for the Englishman it
was a matter of simple trade. Russia represented a
market specially made for English woollens. In its cold
climate the merchants of the " Edward Bonaventure "
found a far readier sale for their goods than they would
have found in the territories of the Great Khan. It is
true that in exchange for their cargo they could not hope
to obtain the jewels and silks and spices on which they
had set their hearts, but Russia offered them useful if less
glamorous products. There were furs—rich sables and
ermine—wax and tallow, sperm oil, hemp and flax.
Chancellor and his companions had the vision and
business sense to see that in the exchange of these
products lay the opportunity for a valuable trade which
in the future might become an important asset to English
commerce.

When spring finally cleared the ice from the landlocked
harbours of the White Sea, the Englishmen returned to
their ship and set sail for England. Chancellor brought
with him a letter from the Czar to Edward VI. It spoke
in the most cordial terms of Chancellor's mission and of
his request for trade. It promised English ships a safe
harbourage in the ports of Russia, and agreed that
English merchants " have their free Marte with all free
liberties through my whole dominions with all kindes

of wares to come and goe at their pleasure, without any let, damage or impediment."

This was the entirely unexpected result of the voyage. Somewhere *en route* the " Edward Bonaventure " was set upon and robbed by Flemish pirates, but the dangers of the stormy passage of the North Cape were successfully overcome and in the summer of 1554 Chancellor landed in London.

But what of Sir Hugh Willoughby and the other two vessels of the fleet which had sailed so gaily past the courtiers and townsfolk of Greenwich some twelve months earlier ? Where had the men of the " Bona Esperanza " and the " Bona Confidentia " been while Chancellor was dining at the Court of the Czar of Russia ? When the " Edward Bonaventure " sailed on its homeward voyage no word of them had been received. When it put into harbour it was discovered that nothing had been heard of them in London. They had simply disappeared on that dark and stormy night when " by violence of winde, and thickenesse of mists " the little fleet had been separated as it fought its way about the North Cape.

It was later in the following summer that some Russian fishermen, sailing along the bleak coast of Lapland, found the two English vessels lying at anchor. There was no sign of life about them. They lay there desolate and strangely quiet. Going on board the Russians came upon a sight that horrified them. The ships were manned by crews of dead men. The sixty-eight seamen who had left London to gather gold in Cathay and spices on the warm shores of the Indies were all there, but every one of them was dead. They had either frozen or starved during the long northern winter.

In a letter of November 4, 1555, the Venetian ambassador in London wrote home " of strange things about

the mode in which they were frozen . . . some of them
seated in the act of writing, pen still in hand, and the
paper before them, others at tables, platter in hand and
spoon in mouth ; others opening a locker, and others
in various postures, like statues, as if they had been
adjusted and placed in those attitudes."

Among Willoughby's possessions brought back to
England was found a copy of his will, which showed that
he and probably some of his men had lived until January
before overtaken by their fate. There was also discovered the log of his ship, which gives us some idea of
the English seamen's lost and bewildered wanderings
before they were frozen in.

On that night of storm after they had been driven out
to sea, the " Bona Confidentia " and the " Bona
Esperanza " completely lost their bearings. When
morning dawned the seamen had no idea of where they
were, and no way of finding Vardo, where they might
hope to meet the " Edward Bonaventure " and its more
experienced navigators. So they sailed north and east
for fourteen days. At last they came upon land. What
it was we are not sure, probably Novaya Zemlya,
although for years the maps of these seas were to be
marked with a mysterious island known as Willoughby's
Land. Whatever it was, however, its shores were
inhospitable. Sir Hugh's journal mournfully records
that there was no sign of human life, " no similitude of
habitation."

The two ships next sailed south-west with the idea of
making their way back to civilization, any hope of finding
a passage to Cathay now given up. The cold and grey
seas showed little promise of that temperate channel they
had dreamed of discovering. At length on September
18, four months after they had left England, and while
Chancellor was making his way to Moscow, they came
upon more land. It was the coast of Lapland. Going

ashore the seamen found all sorts of wild game—seals,
bears, deer, foxes and "divers straunge beasts, as
guloines, and such other which were to us unknowen,
and also wonderfull." They spent a week exploring
the shore and hunting, and then prepared to set out again
with the hope of rounding the North Cape and reaching
familiar waters.

It was too late. Already " very evill wether, as frost,
snow, and haile, as though it had been the deepe of
winter," was upon them. The seas would soon be
frozen over. Willoughby and his men came to the
inevitable decision that there was nothing to do under
these unfavourable circumstances but prepare to winter
just where they were. In one last effort to get in touch
with the world Sir Hugh sent off three men to the south-
east. After three days they returned to the ships, again
" without finding of people, or any similitude of
habitation."

That tragic phrase ! and for the last time. It was with
this entry that Willoughby closed his journal. The rest
is silence, as the men so pitifully imprisoned in their
ships, with no idea of how to prepare for the rigours of
an Arctic winter, slowly froze to death.

CHAPTER IV

TRADE WITH MUSCOVY

IT was a changed England to which Chancellor returned in the summer of 1554. A fateful year had marked his absence in Muscovy. King Edward had for the last time showed his wan face at the windows of his palace at Greenwich, in order to assure his subjects that he was still alive. Conspiracy had given Lady Jane Grey her brief hour on the British throne. And finally, as rightful heir, Mary had been proclaimed Queen amid the general rejoicing of a people who little realized how soon the streets of London were to be lined with gibbets as their sovereign ruthlessly stamped out the rebellion of her enemies.

Even more important, Mary had consummated her Spanish marriage, and Philip had landed earlier in the summer to meet his bride at Winchester. With him had come the Duke of Alva and four thousand Spanish cavaliers ; but the English crowds who lined the streets to see this gay cavalcade pass by on its way to the palace had muttered ominously. They did not welcome these enemies of their country and henchmen of the Pope. They saw in Mary's match the threat of a foreign yoke and an attack upon English liberties.

Yet despite the uncertainties of the political situation the return of the " Edward Bonaventure," with reports of a new trade with Muscovy, created a great sensation in London. Even though Cathay had not been found, here was promise of a market for English cloth. And

whether Edward, or Lady Jane Grey, or Philip and
Mary were on the English throne, this was England's
great need in the middle of the sixteenth century. Her
economic life was going through a transformation which
demanded an expansion of trade. This was more
important than politics in the minds of London's far-
sighted merchants.

They recognized that Chancellor had performed a
very real service for his country. He had shown himself
to be that rare and excellent man whom Clement Adams
had praised. Those virtues which the year before were
" appearing and shining to the world " had grown " to
the great honour and advancement of this kingdome."

With enthusiasm and high confidence the men who
had sent him out in 1553 now laid their plans for the
future. Early in 1555 they obtained a royal charter
from Philip and Mary confirming their privileges and
granting them a monopoly of the new trade. In so far
as the North was concerned this document bid defiance
to the Papal Bull which might have questioned England's
title to her discoveries. The merchant adventurers
were given " ful and free authoritie, libertie, facultie
and licence, and power to saile to all portes, regions,
dominions, territories, landes, Isles, Islands, and coastes
of the sea, wheresoever before their late adventure or
enterprise unknowen." They were empowered to land,
occupy and acquire title " of our further royall favour
and munificence, of our mere motion, certaine knowledge, and speciall grace." It was especially stipulated
that the territory of Russia and all lands to the northward,
north-eastward, and north-westward " by sea shall not
be visited, frequented, nor hanted by any our subjects,
other then of the sayd company and felowship."

On the rolls of the reorganized company were now
the names of some of the highest dignitaries of the realm.
The Marquis of Winchester, Lord High Treasurer, the

Earl of Arundel, Lord Steward of the Household, the Earl of Bedford, Keeper of the Privy Seal, Lord Howard of Effingham, Lord High Admiral, all bore witness to the importance with which the Russian trade was regarded. One of the charter members of the company was Sir John Gresham, a Lord Mayor of London; another his nephew, Sir Thomas Gresham, the founder of the Royal Exchange; and, still another, Sir William Cecil, who was to be Elizabeth's Secretary of State. The services he had already performed won a charter membership for Chancellor. And finally, as " chiefest setter forth of this journey or voyage," the aged Sebastian Cabot was appointed governor of the Muscovy Company for life.

To control the affairs of this organization which in all totalled some two hundred men—and three women! —there was appointed a council of twenty-eight, selected from " the most sad, discreete, and honest persons of the saide fellowship."

It was planned to send two ships on a second voyage, the " Edward Bonaventure " and a new vessel named the " Philip and Mary." There was no question as to the commander of the expedition. Chancellor had fully earned the right to be appointed " grande Pilot of this fleete," and the affairs of the company were unhesitatingly placed in his hands. The letter he bore from England's rulers to the Duke of Muscovy referred to him as " our right wellbeloved Richard Chancelour," and requested the Czar to continue the " princely favour and goodnesse " which he had shown to the English pilot on his first venture.

Chancellor's instructions were to enter into negotiations for a further confirmation of the trading privileges he had brought back with him the previous year, and to establish headquarters for the English trade wherever possible. Nor was the object of his first voyage

altogether forgotten : " Item, it is to be had in minde, that
you use all wayes and meanes possible to learne howe
men may passe from Russia, either by land or by sea
to Cathaia."

On May 1 he set sail. The voyage about the North
Cape was successfully made this time and both ships
put into Vardo. Here the " Philip and Mary " remained to take on a cargo of fish and sperm oil while
the "Edward Bonaventure" continued alone to the
White Sea. On June 23 it arrived off the mouth of
the Dvina.

The cloth and sugar with which the " Edward Bonaventure " was freighted were then started on their way
to Moscow by river boat, but at the town of Vologda,
where overland travel began, it was found necessary to
abandon them temporarily. The roads were deep in
mud and mire. It was almost impossible to travel,
and Chancellor decided that it was better to place the
goods in storage until snow and cold weather made it
possible to bring them on by sled. Leaving behind
Richard Gray, one of the two merchants whom the
company had sent out to act as its agents in Russia,
Chancellor pushed on to Moscow with four men,
including the second company agent, George Killingworth. They reached the capital on October 4. No
sooner had the Czar heard of their arrival than he saw
to it that they were comfortably housed and sent them
a supply of hens and wine, together with " a poore
fellow to make cleane our house."

Within a few days the Englishmen were summoned
to the Kremlin, and with great cordiality Ivan Vassilivitch took his friend, Richard Chancellor, by the hand
and made him and his companions again welcome.
The Czar's former friendliness towards the English had
in no way abated. They were invited to stay that very
night for a royal banquet.

It was all an old story for Chancellor, but his companions gaped with astonishment when they saw the countless tables groaning under their burden of massive gold and silver plate. The English were seated in the very centre of the room facing the Czar. Throughout the banquet Ivan sent them a succession of gifts from his own table, choice wines and dressed meat, which he particularly favoured. Whenever the names of England's sovereigns were mentioned, the whole company politely rose.

As the Czar finally bade them good night and personally gave to each of them a last cup of wine, he noted the great, golden beard of George Killingworth, which reached out over the table as the Englishman leaned forward for his wine. Ivan took it in his hand and " pleasantly delivered it to the Metropolitane, who seeming to blesse it, sayd in Russe, this is Gods gift." And indeed it was, if we may believe the chronicler of the story, for he declares it was five feet two inches long !

Ivan's cordiality towards the Englishmen did not end with these expressions of his favour. He was as keen as ever for trade, and a conference was immediately arranged between two of his councillors and the English envoys. The result was all that could have been desired. With royal approval England was granted unrestricted trading privileges throughout Russia without the imposition of customs duties or tolls of any sort. Her merchants were to be allowed to buy and sell at either retail or wholesale, to pass through the country at will, and, most important of all, they were to be permitted to govern themselves and their affairs according to their own laws.

Three cities were determined upon where they might set up those " factories," or trading posts equipped with warehouses and homes for resident merchants, through

which all foreign trade was carried on at this time. The
first of them was Kholmogory, a town near the mouth
of the Dvina, which was the mart to which the half-
savage Lapps, the idol-worshipping Samoyedes, and the
Karelians came every winter with their reindeer sledges
loaded with salt, stockfish, salmon, sperm oil, furs and
walrus teeth. It was on the advice of Ivan's chancellor
that the English established themselves here, and after
the Czar had granted them some land they built in
Kholmogory "faire houses with offices for their com-
moditie very many."

The second centre of trade was Vologda, the inland
city where the English had already had occasion to store
their goods. It was noted for its tallow and bacon, its
hemp and flax. The new-comers hoped to divert to
this market the trade which might otherwise go to the
Flemish merchants at Novgorod. The company's headquarters were established at the third city, which was of
course Moscow. It was not as important a place for
trade as the other two, although the Czar himself dabbled
in the new commerce and exchanged hemp and flax for
English wool, but it was essential for the company to have
a representative at the Russian Court. Ivan gave the
English a house near the Church of St. Maxim and
almost adjoining the house of Nikita Romanoff, grandfather of the first of the Romanoff Czars.

These arrangements made, the "Edward Bonaventure"
soon sailed for home. It took back the most optimistic
reports of the possibilities of the Russian trade and one
tragic item of news which we already know. The
fishermen of the Lapland coast had reported to the Czar
their strange discovery of two English ships locked in,
the ice far to the north. England could no longer
cling to the hope that the failure of Sir Hugh Willoughby
to return with Chancellor meant that he had discovered
the passage to the East. As it was later to be written of

the Jesuit traveller, Benedict Goes, seeking Cathay he had found heaven.

Chancellor did not go back with his ship. He stayed that winter in Moscow, as he had in 1553–54. Unfortunately we know little of his activities. Russian records speak of his many virtues and the admirable restraint he exercised over his fellow-countrymen, but his own account for that year was tragically lost. He did, however, continue to hold the confidence of the Czar and interested him more and more in the English trade. Political ideas were also brewing in the royal head. Ivan was in many respects the forerunner of Peter the Great. Like his more famous successor, his eyes were turned toward the West, and he hoped to raise his country from the sloughs of barbarism by drawing upon European civilization. The opening of trade with England was his first opportunity to develop his tenuous contacts with Western Europe and to establish communications which could not be blocked by Russia's traditional enemies, Poland and Lithuania. Chancellor undoubtedly encouraged him in these ideas, for the Czar decided before the Englishman's departure to despatch an ambassador under his care to the English Court.

While Chancellor was thus promoting England's interests in Russia with both tact and energy, the merchants in London were planning a third voyage. The "Edward Bonaventure" and the "Philip and Mary" were to sail again with extra crews to attempt to salvage Willoughby's two ships, and at the same time Stephen Burroughs, who had been Chancellor's captain on his first voyage, was to be sent in the pinnace "Serchthrift," on another venture to find the North-east Passage.

The latter voyage was not too successful. Sailing north and east the "Serchthrift" sighted Novaya Zemlya, the islands of Vaigach, and the land of the Samoyedes. Here for some curious reason one of the crew was left

THE KREMLIN

From "Voyages de Corneille le Brun par la Moscovie, en Perse, et aux Indes Orientales, 1718"

to return later to Moscow with strange tales of the devilish
rites of these idolaters who lived in deerskin tents and
were believed to eat the unwary Russians who visited
their shores. The "Serchthrift" had planned to go on
to the mouth of the River Ob, whence tales had come of
the "most sweete harmonie of bels in the lake of Kitthay."
But the hope of finding here the passage to the East
again proved illusory. On August 22 snow fell so
heavily that it had to be shovelled off the decks, and the
"Serchthrift" was blocked "because of great and terrible
abundance of ice." Burroughs was forced to give up all
idea of voyaging further, and instead turned his ship
back toward the West and the safety of a Russian harbour.

In the meantime the "Edward Bonaventure" and the
"Philip and Mary" had reached the Dvina. Their
cargoes of woollens, Hampshire kerseys, linen cloth in
all colours, pewter and sugar were successfully exchanged
for sperm oil, tallow, wax, hemp, yarn, felt, flax and furs.
These products were the staples of the Anglo-Russian
trade. Furs might have been expected to bulk largest
in this list, but before long the company's agents were
instructed to send "no great plentie." There was not
much demand for them in London. "As for Sables
and other rich Furres," wrote the merchants, "they bee
not every mans money."

The company centred its trade on naval supplies.
There was a constantly growing need for them in England,
as more ships were being built all the time, and very good
profits could be realized on their importation. In time
the company was to send its own apprentices to set up
a rope factory at Kholmogory. It must be admitted
that the English made the most of their opportunities
in the new commerce. The Russian merchants had little
idea of the cost of foreign goods, and the company's
agents often charged them two and three times the normal
value of the English woollens and linens.

3

By the summer of 1556 Chancellor was ready to return
to England. The "Bona Esperanza" and the "Bona
Confidentia" had been recovered and manned with extra
crews. The "Edward Bonaventure" and the "Philip
and Mary" were fully loaded, not only with the cargo
of the English merchants but with some £6,000 worth of
goods, which a group of ten Russian merchants were
taking to England on their own account.

With Chancellor, on the "Edward Bonaventure,"
sailed a distinguished guest. Osep Napea, the governor
of Vologda, accompanied him as first Russian ambassador
to the English Court. He bore as royal gifts to Philip
and Mary a pair of hunting falcons with mounted fittings,
some live sables, and a selection of costly furs.

Leaving Russia on July 20, all went well with the four
vessels until they reached the coast of Norway. Here
they ran into terrific weather, which recalled to Chancellor only too vividly the storms which he had met on
that first venture about the North Cape. The ships
were scattered by the sudden fury of the sea and scudded
before the wind in an attempt to reach a safe haven at
the Norwegian port of Trondhjem.

The "Philip and Mary" made harbour in safety,
although it was not until the next spring that London
learned of its fate, but the ill-omened "Bona Confidentia"
and "Bona Esperanza" were not so fortunate. The
former ran on rocks at the very entrance to the harbour
and went down with all hands ; the latter was never
heard from again. As for the "Edward Bonaventure,"
it seemed for a while to bear a charmed life. It rode
out this storm successfully, and with Chancellor and
the Russian ambassador aboard sailed on alone toward
the Scottish coast, as in 1553 it had sailed alone to the
north-east.

It was a rough passage to the shores of Aberdeen-
shire, however ; and, when after almost four months

Chancellor caused the anchor to be dropped off Pitsligo, the seamen of the " Edward Bonaventure " were able to breathe freely for the first time since leaving the White Sea. The storm-wracked ship seemed to be safe at last. Yet that very night, the night of November 10, 1556, another storm swept down from the north. The ship snapped its cables and crew and passengers found themselves drifting helplessly toward the rocky coast.

Chancellor's first thought was for the safety of the Russian ambassador whom the Czar had entrusted to his care. He decided to launch a small boat. They put off in the inky darkness, " using all carefulnesse for the safetie of the bodie of the sayde Ambassador and his trayne," and as the " Edward Bonaventure " was dashed against the cliffs they struggled in the pounding surf to land their boat. For a while it seemed that they would succeed. Then with safety almost in their grasp, with the keel grounding on the shore, a final wave swept over them and the boat was swamped.

By some miracle the Russian ambassador and several of his suite were saved, but not Chancellor. " By rigorous waves of the seas, he was by darke night overwhelmed and drownded."

So at the very height of his career the life of this pioneer in English trade and discovery, this " worthy of aeternall good fame and grateful memory," was cut short. But not before he had laid the foundation of Anglo-Russian friendship and pointed the path to the overseas expansion of English trade.

" Wil it not in all posteritie be as great a renowne unto our English nation," the loyal Hakluyt asked in 1598, " to have been the first discoverers of a Sea beyond the North Cape (never certainly knowen before) and of a convenient passage into the huge Empire of Russia by way of the Bay of St. Nicholas and the river Dvina ; as for the Portingales to have found a sea beyond the

Cape of Buona Esperanza and so consequently a passage by Sea into the East Indies ; or for the Italians and Spaniards to have discovered unknowen lands so many hundred leagues westward and south-westward of the streets of Gibraltar ? "

If posterity has not seen fit to place the name of Richard Chancellor beside those of Diaz, Vasco da Gama, Columbus, Balboa and John Cabot, we may be glad that his own age was more generous.

II

ANTHONY JENKINSON, *died* 1611

" A man of rare vertue, great travaile and experience."
SIR HUMPHREY GILBERT.

CHAPTER V

THE ROAD TO BOKHARA

FATAL or successful, the voyages to the north-east were beginning to whet England's appetite for further trade and discovery. In the spring of 1557 not one of the Muscovy Company's vessels had returned safely. Two of the four ships were known to be lost; there was little hope for the others. Yet the merchants of London had no hesitation about sending out another expedition. No matter how many lives were sacrificed in the attempt to reach the East, there were always more men to fill the places of those who disappeared into the unknown. On May 12, 1557, four new vessels sailed from Gravesend.

Their goal was no further than the White Sea and the merchants aboard them were bound for Muscovy, but the commander of the expedition had other instructions. Anthony Jenkinson, "a man well travelled, whom we mind to use in further travelling," was to go on from Moscow and seek by land the passage to Cathay which neither Willoughby nor Chancellor had been able to find by sea. The Russian trade was important and valuable, but the London merchants still dreamed of a richer and more glamorous commerce than that in which woollens were exchanged for hemp and flax and tallow.

Jenkinson was a merchant and a seaman. He had made his way—how we do not know—through all of Europe and along the eastern shores of the Mediterranean. In 1553 he had been in Aleppo when Solyman the Magnificent marched into that city with an army of 300,000 men and 200,000 camels on his way to war against the Persians. Otherwise all we know of Jenkinson's early life is that he had been trained as a merchant by an apprenticeship which had carried him from Flanders to Tripoli, from Portugal to the Holy Land, and that in 1555 he had become a member of the Mercers' Company.

For his voyage to Russia he received instructions much the same as those which Sebastian Cabot had given the first expedition. Particularly was he warned of the need to keep his fleet together. " If miste or darke weather " should separate the ships, " the Admiral shal make sound and noise by drumme, trumpet, horne, gunne or otherwise or meanes." Furthermore, Jenkinson was to be on his guard lest " treachery, invasion, or other perill of molestation be done or procured to be attempted to our ships by any kinges, princes, or companies, that do mislike this new found trade by seas to Russia." The Muscovy Company had every intention of protecting its dearly-bought monopoly.

Aboard the " Primrose," the flagship of this fleet, was the Russian ambassador. After his miraculous rescue from the wreck of the " Edward Bonaventure " Osep Napea had made his way to London and been warmly welcomed by the English merchants engaged in the Russian trade. The Lord Mayor and his aldermen had ridden out to meet this envoy of the Muscovites in all the glory of their scarlet robes of state. He had been received in audience by Philip and Mary. Now he was returning to Moscow with gifts for the Czar which the old chronicler in Hakluyt tells us included cloth of scarlet, violet and azure, and " a Male and Female Lions."

The course first plotted by Chancellor was easily followed by Jenkinson, and after a passage of just two

JENKINSON'S MAP OF RUSSIA   *From Ortelius "Theatrum Orbis Terrarum"*

months the fleet anchored off the mouth of the Dvina. The Russian ambassador went immediately to Moscow; Jenkinson followed more leisurely, stopping at both Vologda and Kholmogory. Part of his journey was by boat and part by sled. He arrived at the capital early in December and on Christmas Day was received by the Czar.

As soon as spring set in Jenkinson sought from Ivan permission to carry out the real object of his mission. It was to proceed overland through the Czar's territories, and those of the Tartar princes who had but recently been brought under the Russian yoke, with the idea of discovering the old mediæval trail to the East. In the past there had been three main routes for the exchange of the products of East and West. One of them led through Central Asia to the basin of the Caspian. Jenkinson hoped to find this trail, and when the Czar's ready permission was granted he set out with two English companions, a Tartar interpreter and a consignment of English cloth, with no more definite objective than Cathay and the lands of the Great Khan. [6]

The little party left Moscow on April 23, and first made its way to Novgorod. Here it joined forces with the staff of a Russian official, who was going south to take up his post as governor of the newly conquered territory of Astrakhan, and together the travellers took boat down the Volga. The country through which they passed was ravaged by famine and plague. The fierce bands of Nogai Tartars, once in proud alliance with the Eastern Empire, were now torn asunder by civil strife. They lived a restless, nomadic life, moving their houses about on carts drawn by camels, and with " delight in no arte nor science, except the warres " spent their time in raiding their enemies.

As they neared Astrakhan after almost three months' travel the English found the results of plague and famine

even worse than on the steppes. The streets of the
city were blocked with heaps of dead. The Russian
officials, busy setting up their new government, paid
little or no attention to the Tartars who came in from the
country to die of starvation on their doorsteps. Jenkinson reported that he could have bought children by the
thousand for sixpence-worth of bread, but added that
he " had more need of victualles at that time then of any
such merchandize."

From Astrakhan he was entering upon territory
entirely unknown to the English, the Moslem states of
Central Asia. It was a hazardous undertaking which
would have been absolutely impossible for most
Europeans, but Jenkinson possessed unusual resourcefulness. Although he spoke none of the languages of
the people with whom he came in contact, he was able
to enlist their services to help him on his way, and to
command their loyalty to an amazing degree. He
probably won their confidence by the adoption of many
native customs. He tells us for instance how he had
been recognized by the Czar when he appeared at the
Court in Moscow in " Russe apparel." Yet this, of
course, explains very little. It was something in Jenkinson, and not in the clothes he wore, which made it
possible for him to win the favour of the Moslem princes
with whom he was to come in contact.

We shall see that he was, above all, brave and fearless.
But what most enabled him to travel successfully seems
to have been the single fact that travel was the passion
of his life. His zest for seeking out the unknown was
unusual even in that age of discovery. He was ready
to follow any path to the East wherever it might
lead, no matter through what danger it might take
him.

The next stage of his journey was to cross the Caspian,
and for this short voyage he joined with some Tartar

and Persian merchants to buy a small barque. Jenkinson took the helm himself and after navigating successfully down the reaches of the Volga they sailed for some days along the northern shore of the great inland sea. Off the mouth of the Ural the Englishman had his first taste of the dangers threatening a Christian venturing so deep into Moslem lands.

The barque was anchored and all of its crew and passengers were ashore except five Tartars and Jenkinson, who was lying in bed " sore sick." Suddenly a band of thirty armed men appeared and boarded the ship. They declared they had come to kill and rob the infidels who they knew were on the vessel. Defence was impossible. There was nothing Jenkinson could do; but faced by such a crisis his Tartar seamen swore with astounding oaths that there were no Christians aboard the barque.

A little while after this incident storms drove the ship ashore and the travellers found themselves among some Turkomans, who promised them protection. But it was protection of rather doubtful value. Before long Jenkinson realized that these people were really " very badde and brutishe." They " ceased not dayly to molest us," he wrote, " either by fighting, stealing or begging, raysing the price of horses and camels, and victuals double . . . they forced us to buy the water that wee did drinke."

Nevertheless he reached an agreement with them through which a thousand camels were provided to carry the goods of both the English and Tartar merchants. This enabled the little party to abandon their barque and go on by caravan. Within a few days the English learned, however, that the thievery to which they had had to submit at the hands of the Turkomans was the rule of the steppes. Their caravan was set upon by the agents of the prince through whose territory they were travelling and their goods plundered at will.

Jenkinson was far from the protection of either his own sovereign or that of the Russian Czar, from whom he bore letters to the Tartar chieftains, but this official depredation seems to have aroused his fighting blood. He straightway " ridde unto the same Prince," protested vigorously against the treatment he had received, and demanded a passport for free trade. The surprised ruler was impressed. This foreign merchant from a land of which he had never heard spoke with spirit and authority. He asked Jenkinson various questions which the latter shrewdly answered " as unto me seemed best." The Moslem prince was still more impressed, and the upshot of the affair was that after he had " intertained me very greatly, commanding mee to be well feasted with flesh and mares milk," the Prince presented Jenkinson with a horse and the passport he had demanded.

Despite this unexpected hospitality, Jenkinson left the princely presence, " very glad that I was gone," and hurriedly rejoined the caravan.

They now travelled for twenty days through the desert lands which lie beyond the Caspian on the road to the East. They found no towns nor habitations of any sort. All of this territory had been rendered desolate by the tribal warfare of the Tartar chieftains. The great empire formed by Genghis Khan, when his Mongol hordes had swept westward to the borders of Europe and exacted their tribute from the princes of Muscovy, had fallen to pieces. In its stead were numberless petty principalities. Once powerful tribes had become mere robber bands which restlessly roamed the steppes and pillaged the countryside. No caravan was safe from their attack.

The Tartar tribesmen were a lawless race whose lone virtues were bravery and good horsemanship. When

not harrowing the caravan routes they spent their time
in hunting wild horses, or sitting about their tented
camps dicing and drinking mares' milk. They acknowledged no authority except that of the sword.

For a time Jenkinson's caravan went on in safety
except for the very real danger from the exhaustion of
its supplies. The travellers were forced to eat a camel
and a horse. Their water was all but gone before they
reached the khanate of Khiva, where new provisions
could be obtained. The ruler of this territory, Hadjim
Khan, summoned Jenkinson to his Court. Again the
adventurous Englishman gave a good account of himself.
He presented his letters from the Russian Czar, paid
certain duties on his English goods, and won a safe
conduct into the neighbouring khanate of Urgendj.

It was shortly after leaving this latter place that the
caravan had its most narrow escape. Four Tartar spies
were discovered one night in the travellers' camp, and
from these men it was learned that a robber band was
lying in wait to attack the caravan. The intrepid
Jenkinson immediately sought out the local prince,
whose grandiloquent title was the Sultan of Kath, and
demanded protection.

A guard was provided upon his demand for a safe
passage, but within a few days these supposed friends
demanded tribute for themselves. Jenkinson flatly refused. He rightly decided that the Sultan's soldiers
and the bandits were in league and that the caravan
would have to rely upon its own strength.

The situation was serious, and the Englishman's
Moslem companions asked that they might halt while
the ceremony of sacrificing a sheep was performed
to determine what the Fates willed. Their sorceries
revealed that the caravan would meet thieves but would
overcome them. That night the forty members of the
party, their courage renewed by this portent, swore a

solemn oath that they would fight and if necessary die together.

They did not have long to wait before the bandits attacked. Under Jenkinson's lead the caravan was drawn up in a hollow square with camels and men protected as far as possible by piles of goods and supplies. And then " from morning untill two hours within the night " the desert battle raged. The bandits were keen marksmen, and sweeping past on their wild Tartar horses sent thick flights of arrows into the beleaguered camp, but Jenkinson and his two English companions had more deadly weapons in their English arquebuses. This saved the day. When darkness fell the robbers withdrew and sent an envoy to ask for a truce and a parley.

The Moslem chief of the caravan was sent out to talk with him. In the stillness of a clear, starlit night the Englishmen could hear every word of the parley on which their fate depended. The bandits' proposal was simple : surrender the Christians and we will leave you in peace. Jenkinson and his companions must have listened fearfully for their envoy's answer. Their hearts must have leaped at his stout statement that he had no Christians in his caravan, and " although hee had, hee would rather die then deliver them."

The answer of the bandits was to drag the loyal Moslem off to their camp. Again the English must have felt that all was lost. They knew their envoy would be maltreated and perhaps tortured to confess that there were Christians in the caravan. Yet there was nothing they could do. They were completely in his hands.

The Moslem proved faithful to his companions. He gave nothing away, and as morning came the travellers were ready to renew the battle for their lives and property. But the bandits had had about enough of the withering fire from the English arquebuses. They despaired of capturing the caravan and offered to let it pass if it would pay tribute of a camel and " 20 times 9 severall things." The English and their Moslem allies, " loth to go to battel againe," decided to accept this proposal.

After the deal had been made the bandits withdrew and the travellers hurried on, leaving the regular caravan route to pass " through a wilderness of sand " in the hope of avoiding any further attacks. That same night they reached the comparative safety of the bank of the River Oxus.

A few days later there was another alarm. More spies were discovered and " there was a greate shoute and cry." " We immediately laded our camels," writes Jenkinson, " and departed, being about midnight and very darke." This time they " drove sore " until their safety was really assured and thereafter clung closely to the river bank. On December 23, five months after they had launched their barque at Astrakhan and started eastward, " we arrived at the citie of Boghar in the land of Bactria." ·

Boghor was Bokhara. It was—and still is—one of the world's oldest cities. Some centuries earlier it had been one of the great capitals of Central Asia. Flourishing under the rule of the Arabs, Bokhara had been captured and burned by Genghis Khan, only to rise from its ashes in the days of Timur the Lame. Here the Polo brothers had spent three years on their overland journey to Cathay in the thirteenth century. A great walled and gated city, its fame had spread even to the Western world. Bokhara and the neighbouring city of Samarkand symbolized the riches and romance of the East.

If the Bokhara of 1558 no longer knew the glories of the days before its walls were levelled and its mosques and universities burned to the ground by the avenging

Mongols, it was still a thriving city. It was on the
cross-roads of Asia. Indians from Bengal brought to
Bokhara cambrics and muslins to exchange for the red
hides of Russia ; merchants of Persia brought wool,
linen cloth and the " tall and noble " horses of Argamak ;
in times of peace came caravans from Cathay with satin,
damask, musk and rhubarb. Above all, there was the
slave market. It was the largest in Central Asia. Captive
Persians, fierce, bearded Afghans, peasants of Russia,
and Tartars of the steppes captured in tribal raids, were
here auctioned off to the shrewd Hindu merchants
from beyond the Ganges.

No Englishman had ever been in Bokhara before or
penetrated so far into Central Asia. Jenkinson's long
and dangerous journey along the shores of the Caspian,
across the desert wastes of what is now known as
Turkestan, through territory ravaged by the Tartar
tribesmen, was an exploit which found no parallel in
the story of English travels.

He found Bokhara a city of small earthen houses
but with many temples and monuments of stone " sump-
tuously builded, and gilt, and specially bathstones so
artificially built that the like thereof is not in the worlde."
Some little time before it had been subject to Persia,
but it was now independent, and its king, Abdullah
Khan, was waging incessant and futile war against the
rival kingdom of Samarkand. His rule was autocratic
and tyrannical ; his extortionary taxes on trade kept
him in great wealth.

Two odd things about Bokhara are particularly noted
in Jenkinson's journal. The water of its river bred
" a worme of an ell long " which got into the people's
blood when they used this water for drinking. It was
then " pluckt out about the ancle with great art and
cunning, the Surgeons being much practiced therein,
and if shee breake in plucking out, the party dieth, and

every day she commeth out about an inch, which is rolled up, and so worketh till she be all out."

Notwithstanding the unsavoury condition of the drinking water, Jenkinson goes on to say of Bokhara: " It is there forbidden to drinke any other thing then water, & mares milk, and whosoever is found to breake that lawe is whipped and beaten most cruelly through the open markets, and there are officers appointed for the same who have authoritie to goe into any mans house, to search if hee have either aquavita, wine or brage, and finding the same, doe breake the vessels, spoyle the drinke, and punish the masters of the house cruelly, yea, and many times if they perceive but by the breath of a man that he hath drunke, without further examination hee shall not escape their handes." Here was prohibition with a vengeance.

Jenkinson was soon summoned before Abdullah Khan. He presented his letters, explained his mission, and with that uncanny ability to win the confidence of Moslems which we have already seen in at least two instances serving to save his life, became a favourite with this petty prince. There was something about Jenkinson which made an immediate impression upon the half-barbarous khans of Central Asia, some combination of pride and deference which held their respect. But whatever may have been responsible for it, Jenkinson was entertained at Court " most greatly," and the King promptly sent out a hundred of his men to scour the countryside for the bandits who had attacked the caravan.

After several audiences, wrote Jenkinson, Abdullah Khan " devised with me familiarly in his most secret chamber." The Englishman and the Moslem princeling talked of the affairs of Russia, Turkey and England. The Khan showed special curiosity in English methods of warfare and in the visitor's arquebuses. Jenkinson

4

explained all that he could and then " did shoote in
hand gunnes before him, and he did himselfe practise
the use thereof."

Yet, despite this friendship and this intimate target
practice, Jenkinson found that he made a mistake when
he sold some of his English cloth to the King.   He was
forced to record that Abdullah Khan " shewed himselfe
a very Tartar : for he went to the warres owing me
money, and sawe mee not paide before his departure."

Jenkinson's purpose in coming to Bokhara, however,
was not primarily to establish friendly relations with
Abdullah Khan, but to trade and to seek the route to
Cathay.   Sadly enough he found little sale for English
goods in this Central Asian market.   The cloth which
he had so laboriously brought about the North Cape,
across the whole of Russia and the Caspian Sea, along the
caravan trails of the southern steppes, had been brought
those thousands of miles in vain.   Indian and Tartar
merchants seeking wool found that of England no better
and no cheaper than that of Persia.

And, disappointment even more bitter, there was no
commerce with Cathay.   It was several years since a
caravan had come out of the Far East because of the
wars " that had dured 3. yeeres before my comming
thither."   Tashkend and Kashgar were being attacked
by the roving tribes of Kalmucks and their raids
" stopped up the way " to the East just as effectively
as ice blocked the North-east Passage by sea.   No
caravan could hope to pass along the trail of Marco
Polo, let alone one with merchants of England.

Jenkinson learned how he might make the far journey
if the tribes were at peace.   It was fourteen days to
Tashkend, seven to the Greek ruins of Uzkand, twenty to
Kashgar, thirty to Suh-chau, five to Kan-chau, sixty
more of easy travelling through pleasant and fertile
land to Cathay, and finally five more to Cambuloo, the

SPORT AT AN EASTERN CAPITAL

From Thévenots' "Voyages," 1727

capital of the Great Khan.   Five months from Bokhara
by this reckoning.   There were strange races on the
border of the Khan's empire, Jenkinson was told by
his informers ; a people of tawny colour who worshipped
fire and ate raw flesh, others who were beautiful beyond
words and ate with knives of gold, still others who were
pygmies.   The people of Cathay itself, according to
legend in Bokhara, were " white and of fair complexion
. . . civil and unspeakably rich."

This was all valuable information even though it
was useless at the time.   Jenkinson might hope that
some day English merchants could cross the plains
of Asia, although for himself there was no chance.   He
did not know what to do.   For a while he considered
diverting his course to Persia, but here again there was
so much intermittent fighting between the Persians
and the Tartar tribesmen that " the waies they were
destroied."   Finally war came to drive him out of
Bokhara itself.   Abdullah Khan had led his army
against Samarkand and " newes came, that he was
fled."   His capital was threatened with siege, and with
the whole country in arms no merchant and no caravan
were safe.   Jenkinson feared that he might some day
find himself on the auction block in the Bokhara slave
market.

The decision to retrace his course was inevitable if he
hoped ever to see England again.   With his two English
companions he joined a great caravan of 600 camels,
which was about to set out on the journey back to the
Caspian, and still laden with by far the greater part of his
woollens he left Bokhara on March 8, 1559.   It was just
in time to escape the siege undertaken by the King of
Samarkand.

Ambassadors from the Khans of Bokhara and of
Balkh, accredited to the Czar of Russia, accompanied
him and when he passed through Urgendj four more

envoys were added to his party. In the name of Ivan
the English traveller gave them promises of safety
and agreed to introduce them at the Russian Court,
where they hoped to establish friendly relations with
the all-powerful Czar. Jenkinson had become an emissary of Russia as well as of England and the curious
fate which had made his expedition a commercial
failure for the merchants of London was turning it
into a diplomatic success for the Russian Czar. It was
through Jenkinson that these Tartar tribes made their
first friendly contacts with Muscovy.

The journey across the steppes was marked by only
one bandit attack. The caravan drove off its assailants
and at length reached the shores of the Caspian, where
Jenkinson sought out the barque which he had left
there the year before. He found it without trouble,
but its small boat, its sails, cables and anchor had all
disappeared. With his usual resourcefulness Jenkinson
immediately set his men to work spinning cables,
making sails and fashioning a wooden anchor. His
crew consisted of himself and his two English companions
but the barque carried as passengers the six Tartar
ambassadors and twenty-five Russian slaves whom
Jenkinson had rescued or purchased somewhere on his
travels and was bringing back with him to the safety of
their own land. At their masthead the English flew
their flag—the " redde crosse of S. George."

Once their improvised cable snapped during a sudden
storm and Jenkinson wrote that they were all " looking
for present death." But their good luck held and they
escaped this tragic close to their adventures. On
May 28, almost a year after they had left the Russian
port, they anchored at Astrakhan.

Here the indefatigable Jenkinson once again tried to
sell his precious cloth. But still there was no market
for it. He soon had to abandon the attempt and with

100 gunners provided by the Czar as a special escort
set out for Moscow.   He reached the capital on September 2 and summoned before Ivan " kissed his hand
and presented him a white Cowes taile of Cathay, and a
drumme of Tartaria, which he well accepted." [7]

As we have already noted, Jenkinson's journey was
one unparalleled in the history of English travel.
Writing of it to Henry Lane, one of the English agents
in Russia, the traveller himself spoke of it as " miserable,
dangerous and chargeable with losses, charges and
expenses, as my penne is not able to expresse the same."
Yet it was to prove a venture of very real significance for
English commerce.   Like Chancellor, who in failing
to find Cathay had discovered Russia and started a
prosperous trade, Jenkinson had failed to reach the
land of the Great Khan but had found potential markets
for English goods among the cities of Southern Russia
and the basin of the Caspian.   He had extended the
limits of the Western world and could accurately report
to London the commercial possibilities of territories
hitherto completely unknown.

CHAPTER VI

THE GREAT SOPHIE

WHEN Jenkinson returned to London in the following spring, after an absence of three years, he found Elizabeth on the throne. The Virgin Queen, before the end of whose reign England was at last to reach the Indies, was vitally interested in everything that could be done to expand English trade. Jenkinson must have been a man after her own heart. His insatiable curiosity for the unknown, his experience and daring in travel, and his sturdy English independence were qualities which Elizabeth appreciated and knew how to reward. She took him into her service, and before the year was out he was off on another venture. This time he bore royal letters to a sovereign known in England as the Great Sophie, or more officially as the Emperor of the Persians, Medes, Parthians, Hyrcanes, Carmanians and Margians.

Jenkinson had not, however, deserted the service of the Muscovy Company. According to the custom of that day he was both its agent and the envoy of his Queen. The merchants of London had rewarded him for his pioneering in Central Asia by making him a member of their company. On this second trip they showed their confidence in his abilities by giving him free rein to go anywhere he thought advisable in his search for new trade. In its instructions the Company spoke of Jenkinson's " approved wisedome with your experience, and also your carefull and diligent minde in the atchieving and bringing to good successe (by the helpe of almighty God) all thinges that you take in hand."

Elizabeth's letters were addressed not only to the Great Sophie but to the Russian Czar. In those to the latter she spoke of " our faithfull, and beloved servant, Anthonie Jenkinson," and requested Ivan to show again " unto the same Anthonie, now admitted into our service, the like favour as heretofore your Majestie of your meere motion, did exhibit unto him being then a private person." Her note to the Persian emperor requested trading privileges which her envoy was authorized to seek in her name for the mutual benefit of England and Persia.

Jenkinson sailed on May 14, 1561, in the " Swallow." August found him in Moscow. For several days, however, he was unable to inform the Czar of his arrival because Ivan was in the midst of the celebrations attendant upon his second marriage. Like everyone in Moscow, except for a few members of the royal household, he was not even permitted to leave his house during the period of festivities.

When the marriage ceremonies were over he sent word of his presence to the Kremlin, but for the first time in his Russian experience he was not invited to Court. He had incurred the enmity or jealousy of Ivan's chief secretary, and for reasons he could not fathom was even refused permission to proceed to Persia. So decided was the prohibition against his further travels that Jenkinson felt that there was nothing to do but return to London. His passports were ready, the post-horses ordered, when Osep Napea, the Russian ambassador with whom he had sailed on his first voyage, unexpectedly intervened. He told the Englishman that he was sure the Czar must have been misinformed of his plans and begged him to wait a few days longer while he investigated what had happened at Court.

Within three days the whole matter was cleared up.
The Czar had been misinformed. His friendship for
the Englishman who had performed such useful services
for him in Central Asia had not wavered. Not only was
Jenkinson given permission to go on to Persia, but he
was entrusted by the Czar with certain special missions.

He left Moscow in company with a Persian ambassador
returning to his own country, and as on his previous
journey made his way down the Volga to Astrakhan
and the Caspian Sea. Here two brigantines were provided by the Russians to make his passage to the Persian
coast a far simpler matter than his hazardous voyage
when *en route* to Bokhara. They made one stop at
Derbend, where a gigantic citadel which tradition said
had been built by Alexander the Great frowned down
upon the sea, and landed at Shabran.

This city was in Shirvan, once an independent country
but then owing allegiance to the Persian Shah, and soon
after disembarking Jenkinson was summoned to the
capital of the King of Shirvan at Shemakha. Horses
and camels were sent to bring him to the monarch's
summer retreat in the mountains.

Jenkinson found a rich and luxurious camp at the
end of his journey. The royal tents of silver and gold
cloth were set up in a cool glade through which ran a
mountain stream feeding a number of sparkling fountains. The King, another Abdullah Khan, a man of
fierce countenance and forbidding appearance, received
the Englishman cordially and hospitably. He was
dressed in silks, with a most imposing turban. One
end of it, wrote Jenkinson, was turned up a half a yard,
while on the other side of the royal head a plume of
feathers was set ' in a trunke of golde richly inameled.''
Two long pendants of gold hung from his ears. The
King sat cross-legged on a velvet cushion with his
courtiers grouped about him on rich carpets.

Jenkinson first knelt on one knee before this Persian potentate and then tried to seat himself cross-legged on the carpet placed before him. He probably looked uncomfortable in this unnatural position for he writes that " perceiving that it was painefull for me so to sit, his highnesse caused a stoole to be brought in, and did will me to sit thereupon, after my fashion."

According to the customary ceremony of the East a banquet was served almost immediately. There was one course of 140 dishes and then another of 150—Jenkinson counted them. But with all this profusion of Persian delicacies there was no wine. At the conclusion of the banquet Abdullah Khan drank a cup of water taken from one of the fountains, and handing another cup to Jenkinson asked him if there was anything so good in his country. The wily Englishman answered " in such sort, that he was therewith contented."

Jenkinson was soon in the good graces of this monarch to a degree which might surprise us if we had not already had evidence of his popularity among the princes of the East. They talked long of the possible trade between England and the Persian provinces. Abdullah Khan was enthusiastic and promised the Englishman a safe conduct and all possible assistance when he went on to the Court of the Great Sophie. In the meantime he sent him out hawking with his nobles and again invited him to a banquet, which was made the occasion for presenting him with two silk gowns. Jenkinson took off his own velvet cloak and put on these new robes amid the admiration of the assembled Court. The King was merry and Jenkinson in high favour.

When it came time for the English visitor to leave for Kazvin, which the Persian Shah had made his capital after the sack of Tabriz by a Turkish army, Abdullah Khan gave Jenkinson a horse and appointed as his guide

the ambassador with whom he had already travelled
from Moscow.   They left Shemakha on October 6
and in less than a month arrived at Kazvin, having
passed by Baku, a place which even in the sixteenth
century was notable for its petroleum wells, as we read
that near the city " there issueth out of the ground a
marveilous quantitie of oile."

Through no fault of his own Jenkinson had not
chosen a very auspicious time to arrive at Kazvin.
When he reached this city of " evil builded " houses of
sun-dried bricks, the emissaries of the Shah told him
that he must wait some time before presenting his
letters from Elizabeth because " great affaires " were
in hand.

These affairs were nothing less than the celebration
of peace with Turkey.   Shah Tahmasp, a sovereign who
the Englishman found " nothing valiant," although the
magnificence of his Court gave him the character of a
great and mighty prince, had been forced to sue for
peace after the destruction of his capital.   The Turkish
ambassadors had arrived with gifts of gold and horses
valued at £40,000 and a treaty had been signed with
many solemn protestations of friendship.   One of the
nicest phases of the celebration was the Shah's gift to
the Sultan.

The Great Turk had had an undutiful son who had
fled to Persia to escape his father's wrath.   He had been
well received at first, but with the start of the peace
negotiations between Persia and Turkey he had been
thrown into prison.   Now, as a token of amity, the Shah
caused him to be executed and sent his head as a gift to
Constantinople.   It was a present, wrote Jenkinson,
" not a little desired, and acceptable to the unnaturall
father."

This incident may serve as an introduction to Shah
Tahmasp.   A Venetian envoy at his Court has left a

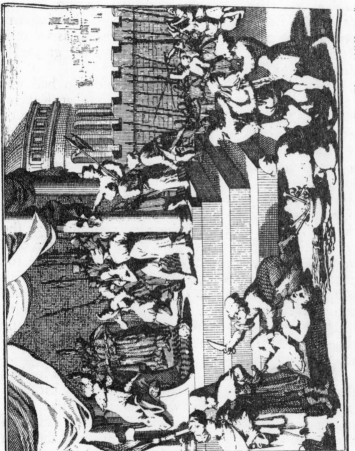

From Thevenot's "Voyages"

JUSTICE AT THE PERSIAN COURT

description of him as an avaricious tyrant fanatically worshipped by the Persian Moslems, members of the Shiah sect, because he was a descendant of Ali, the son-in-law of Mohammed. He was engrossed in the pleasures of his Court, vain and boastful. He lived a secluded life among the 400 wives and concubines which were selected for him from among the fairest virgins of his kingdom.

Two days each week, wrote a later English traveller, these women devoted to the Shah's ablutions. One day they spent " washing, rubbing and bathing him, and the other day in paring his nails, and other matters." In appearance he was a dark, well-formed man of medium height with a short beard and thick, sensual lips. At this time he had been on the throne thirty-eight years.

Perhaps his welcome to Jenkinson would have been more friendly than it proved to be if it had not been for this Turkish treaty he had just concluded. For England and Turkey were not on too cordial terms and the prospect of a direct trade between England and Persia, which might deprive Turkey of the raw silk she imported from Persia by developing an entirely new trade route across the Caspian and up the Volga, would most certainly offend the Shah's new ally. The Turkish merchants in Kazvin had, in fact, lost no time in pointing this out to the Persian ruler. So soon as they had heard of Jenkinson's arrival they had persuaded the Turkish ambassador of the necessity of blocking any English encroachments upon their commerce, and before this envoy had left for Constantinople with the head of the Sultan's rebellious son as a grisly token of Persian friendship, he had taken the matter up with Shah Tahmasp.

Consequently it was without much hope of establishing Anglo-Persian trade relations that Jenkinson appeared at the Persian Court when the Shah finally deigned to

receive him. His account of his reception shows that
his worst fears were realized.

At the gate to the royal palace he was refused entry
for any of his company except one man to serve as an
interpreter, and compelled to put on a pair of special
shoes without which no Giaour—no unbeliever, no
unclean person—was allowed to tread the holy ground
within His Majesty's palace. This was a mark of respect
to " their false filthie prophets " which sorely rankled.

When he was finally brought before the Shah, who sat
in a little gallery above the Court itself, the English
envoy greeted him " with such reverence as I thought
meete to be used." He then explained his mission and
told Tahmasp that he had been sent to Persia by the great
Elizabeth to treat of friendship and trade. He was
asked in what language the Queen's letters were written,
and when he answered that they were in Latin, Italian
and Hebrew, the haughty Shah carelessly replied that
there was no one in his kingdom who could read them.
Jenkinson's diplomatic but shrewd rejoinder was that
" such a famous and worthie Prince (as he was) wanted
not people of all nations within his large dominions to
interprete the same."

This blending of flattery and challenge seems to have
disposed of this problem, for we next find the Shah and
Jenkinson discussing religion. It was a brief and significant argument. The Englishman had to explain carefully that he was neither Mohammedan nor unbeliever,
but a Christian. He had to explain just what were the
Christian beliefs.

Jenkinson himself then records the Shah's summary
decision :

" Dost thou beleeve so sayd the Sophie unto mee :
Yea that I doe sayd I : Oh thou unbeleever sayd he,
we have no neede to have friendship with the unbe-
leevers, and so willed mee to depart."

The Englishman had had enough of the Shah's arrogant questioning and gladly " did reverence " and went his way. His guile might lead him to praise lavishly the hospitality of a friendly prince and answer his questions " in such sort, that he was therewith contended," but it did not shadow his pride and independence before a monarch who challenged either his love for his country or his religious faith. Jenkinson had no idea of grovelling before any man for the sake of English trade. After all, he was an Elizabethan.

The rest of his stay in the Persian capital was marked by intrigue and plotting. He hoped to make some useful contacts with the Indian merchants in Kazvin despite the Shah's displeasure, but the Persian nobles plotted his death. He discovered that they hoped to make a further conciliatory gesture toward Constantinople by an ingenious plan " to send mee with my letters unto the sayde great Turk for a present."

It was only the timely interposition of the friendly King of Shirvan which saved Jenkinson from the fate of the Great Turk's son. This generous prince urged upon his liege lord, Shah Tahmasp, the ill-fame which such a treacherous act would bring upon Persia. Even the all-powerful Emperor of the Medes and Persians, he wrote the Shah, could not execute an ambassador with impunity.

Tahmasp was constrained by this influential intervention to order Jenkinson to leave Kazvin instead of ordering him to be killed, and the Englishman hurriedly fled the capital to find refuge in Shirvan at Abdullah Khan's friendly Court. Here he was fortunate enough to win the trading privileges which he had failed to secure at Kazvin. One of Persia's richest provinces was open for trade, even though the Persian Shah had so abruptly dismissed him. And it was a province famous for its silk.

Another month or two and Jenkinson was on his way back to Russia. While waiting for his boat on the shores of the Caspian an Armenian envoy from the Christian King of Georgia appeared upon the scene seeking aid against the Moslem princes of Persia and Turkey. Jenkinson promised to present his case at the Czar's Court and advised the Georgians to send an envoy of their own to Moscow. Then within two days after the Armenian had left he despatched one of his own company to Georgia to buy silk and seek trading privileges. Jenkinson never missed an opportunity.

On May 30 the returning party arrived at the now familiar Astrakhan and in August reached Moscow. The Czar was well pleased with Jenkinson's conduct of the private business with which he had entrusted him, and told him that he hoped he would again travel in his service.

It was not until September, 1564, that he finally returned safely—" God be praysed "—to London. He had again been away three years and again opened up new paths for English trade.

CHAPTER VII

ENVOY OF ELIZABETH

AFTER his return from Persia the life of Jenkinson
entered upon a new and varied phase. If he
never again travelled on the romantic road to
Bokhara and Samarkand, or staunchly upheld his faith
before the Great Sophie, he continued to play an important rôle in the expansion of English commerce.
Above all, he succeeded in saving the trade of the
Muscovy Company when it was almost lost through the
caprice and anger of Czar Ivan.

It is typical of him that the first thing he did upon
reaching London after the Persian journey was to
petition Queen Elizabeth for authorization to undertake
a new voyage to the North-east. No matter that he
had spent the past seven years in travel; he was ready
to set out again at once. He had not yet reached his
real goal. Moscow, Astrakhan, Bokhara and Kazvin
were but way stations on the route to the Far East. To
find Cathay and the wide and fertile dominions of the
Great Khan had become an obsession with him.

Some of his arguments attempting to prove the
existence of the North-east Passage we have already
heard. They were on the whole much the same as
those which Robert Thorne had advanced half a century
earlier. But Jenkinson was a practical man. He not
only dreamed of the riches of the East, but of markets
for English goods. Experience had taught him that
there was little chance to sell wool in Central Asia,

but he was the more positive it could be sold " in those colde countryes Betwene the Imagyned straighte (of no dowghte to be fownde) and the said Laand of Cathaye."

Jenkinson urged his sovereign eloquently and persuasively to put him in command of a fleet to search out this North-east Passage—" whiche yf I maye lyve to accomplysh I shall attayne the some of my Desyr."

But he was to be disappointed. His dream of sailing to Cathay never materialized. Elizabeth had other work for him to do and we soon find him engaged in a task far different from the search for Eastern gold and spices. He was put in charge of the " Ayde "—a 200-ton ship carrying eighteen guns and 200 men—with orders to suppress piracy along the Scottish coast.

The complaints of the Queen Regent of France, Catherine de Médicis, against attacks on French merchantmen, had forced Elizabeth to take this action, but Jenkinson also carried secret instructions. He was to prevent the landing in Scotland of certain Scottish lords who were conspiring against the projected marriage of Queen Mary and the Earl of Leicester. This soon involved the traveller in political intrigues for which his long absence from England little suited him. Fortunately he was soon recalled to more familiar service.

In the spring of 1566 he was once again sent to represent English interests in Russia. The Muscovy Company was having difficulties with its trade at this period because an Italian adventurer had succeeded in winning Czar Ivan's favour and threatened to undermine England's monopoly in the growing commerce of the White Sea. Jenkinson's mission was to protest in Elizabeth's name against any encroachment upon the English privileges, and to seek a new guarantee from the Czar that " no other straungers may be admytted or lycencyd to land or trade that waye."

When he arrived in Russia he found the state of the

country greatly changed since his last visit. Ivan had entered upon that final phase of his reign which was to earn him his unsavoury title of Ivan the Terrible. In a letter to William Cecil, graphically describing the Russian scene, Jenkinson reported that the Czar " hath used lately great cruelty toward his nobyllyte and gentlemen by puttynge to death, whyppynge, and banyshynge." Four hundred of the boyars had been executed and hundreds more cruelly persecuted. In describing the fate of four of these courtiers Jenkinson wrote : " One wurryed with beares, of another he cutt of his nose, hys tonge, hys eares, and his lyppes, the thyrde was sett upon a pole, and the fourth he commanded to be knocked in the head, and put under the yse in the Ryvar."

Yet despite his tyrannical outbursts and the cruelties which were making his name a byword of terror among his own subjects, the Czar still professed the friendliest feelings for the Englishman who had won his favour on his first appearance at Court. Jenkinson was summoned to the Kremlin within a week of his arrival at Moscow.

In the " very briefe remembrance " which is all the account we have of this trip to Muscovy, Jenkinson simply states that he had much honour done him throughout his stay in Russia. That his mission was successful we have conclusive proof in the new charter which Ivan granted the Muscovy Company. The monopoly of the White Sea trade was definitely reaffirmed and the interfering Italian was banished. (8)

In the winter of 1566–67 Jenkinson may have returned to London by the overland route through Poland and France. We do not know. But that spring a letter from the Muscovy Company to its agents in Russia expressed great dissatisfaction with the way its affairs were being managed and empowered Jenkinson to investigate the situation.

The company listed its complaints at some length. The personal accounts of its representatives were double what they should be and had to be curtailed immediately. Even though it might be the Russian custom to offer wine and meat " to comers and goers to our houses," the English agents had to be more sparing with their hospitality. Nor could the company's apprentices expect London to dress them so they could " ride and goe like lordes." If that was a Russian custom, it also would have to be changed as far as the English were concerned. The company agents were to be forbidden to fix up their houses for ostentation, fancy or pleasure. They were not to be allowed to keep horses, dogs or bears.

Together with these orders for a rigid programme of economy instructions were forwarded to Jenkinson on a more important matter : " Certaine of our servuntes and stipendaries be suspected of horedom, Incontinency, dronchennes and Idellnes ; if they do not amende ship them home."

Affairs were evidently getting out of hand at Moscow, and for the sake of English prestige the London merchants were determined on a thorough reform. Jenkinson was the new broom to sweep the stables clean. The company's letter to its agents definitely stated that " Master Jenkinson who knoweth our mindes in all thinges " was to have a free hand and his orders were to be followed.

When he had successfully carried out this difficult task Jenkinson sailed for England, in the autumn of 1667, bearing a special letter from the Czar for Queen Elizabeth. Certain ideas which Ivan had first considered in his talks with Richard Chancellor had now matured. Hoping that closer political ties would result from the Anglo-Russian trade relations, he asked the English Queen to send an ambassador to his Court. This

tyrannical Czar was to prove that he had something of
the vision of Peter the Great when the matter at hand
was Russia's foreign relations.

Supplementing his official despatch Ivan also entrusted a private message to Jenkinson. This letter
asked that some English shipbuilders and seamen
might be sent to Russia, sought a definite alliance with
England against Poland, and suggested that a secret
clause in the proposed treaty should stipulate that each
nation would provide a sanctuary for the ruler of the
other " yf any mysfortune might fall or chance upon
eyther of theym to goe owt of ther contreys."

Perhaps there was an even more secret message
which Jenkinson was to convey to Elizabeth. The
Czar's predilection for all things English extended to the
Virgin Queen. He was a much-married man, but he
dreamed of still another matrimonial venture with
Elizabeth as his bride. Some time during this period
he broached the subject and there are pretty definite
hints that this was the time. It was certainly natural
for him to entrust such a matter to Jenkinson. In no
other Englishman did he ever have such trust and
confidence.

At all events Jenkinson was charged with an important
and mysterious mission on his return to London, and
the Czar hoped that an answer would be brought him
by one of Elizabeth's high councillors, or, as Jenkinson
himself puts it, " by one of more greater estimacyon
than my self."

The result of the Czar's action was that in June of
the following year Elizabeth sent to Moscow the first
official English embassy credited to the Russian Court.
It was headed by Thomas Randolph, an experienced
diplomat who had already performed various special
services for El'zabeth in her intrigues in Scotland.
There were forty Englishmen in his company, " of

which the one halfe were Gentlemen, desirous to see
the world." Anthony Jenkinson was not of their
number. The significance of this fact we shall soon
see.

Randolph's instructions were vague and general.
Most certainly he was not empowered to say anything
of secret marriage proposals. Nor was he to discuss
the secret clauses of the suggested treaty. Both pro-
positions were highly embarrassing to the Virgin Queen.
Without wishing to offend the Russian Czar, Elizabeth
was not prepared to embrace either his diplomatic or
matrimonial proposals too closely. If the ambassador
was directly questioned on these matters, he was to say
that Elizabeth had felt that Jenkinson must have mis-
understood the Czar's intentions.

"And in such good generall sorte," ran Elizabeth's
orders, " we wold have you satisfie him without giving
occasyon to enter into any speciall Treaties or Capitula-
cion of any such legue as is called offensive and defensive
betwixt us."

Ivan's first reaction upon the arrival of this imposing embassy was bitter disappointment that Jenkinson
was not included in its entourage. If we assume that
the Englishman had been secretly instructed to tell his
Queen of the Czar's matrimonial ambitions, it is easy
to understand that Ivan would interpret his failure to
return to Russia as an almost insulting slight. This
certainly seems to be the logical explanation of the
frantic efforts he made to find out where Jenkinson was
and why he had not come back.

His failure to get any word from his confidant so
enraged him against the English embassy that for a
while Randolph was virtually imprisoned in Moscow—
then the scene of daily and bloody executions of the Czar's
enemies. Finally more sober counsels prevailed and
the ambassador was courteously received. Apparently

Ivan was satisfied with his evasive promises of English interest and support, but he decided to press his treaty proposal by sending his own ambassador back to London with the returning Englishmen. One Andrew Savin was selected for this post, one of his most specific instructions being to request Elizabeth to send Jenkinson on to Moscow.

The negotiations in London did not make any more headway than had those in Moscow. Ivan began to realize that Elizabeth was simply putting obstacles in his path and when in 1570 Savin returned without Jenkinson, without a treaty, and with tales of discourteous treatment in England, he became furious.

There was little diplomatic reserve in the letter he now despatched to Elizabeth. He demanded information of Jenkinson and told of the fruitless attempts he had made to find him or to learn of his whereabouts. He complained of the treatment his ambassador had received in London and grew abusive about Elizabeth's disregard of his friendly advances. He taunted her with being ruled by " bowrish Marchaunts " instead of ruling in her own right, and as a final barbaric fling referred insultingly to her " maydenlie estate."

To strike more directly at this nation of traders he promptly and without any warning annulled the privileges of the Muscovy Company and seized all their property in Russia.

Here was a crisis. Elizabeth might feel that she had been outrageously treated by this half-mad Russian Czar, but she could ill afford to have one of England's most profitable sources of trade completely shut off. By some means Ivan had to be placated. There was only one way this could be done. The Queen turned to Jenkinson.

Why had he not been sent back to Russia before? Where had he been during the past four years? Neither

question can be answered definitely. Apparently Elizabeth had felt that the best way to answer the Czar's
proposals—whether of a secret treaty or of matrimony
—was to ignore them. And this was possible only so
long as Jenkinson was kept out of the way. She had
probably given him some commission which would
keep him both out of Russia and out of England, for
somewhat later Jenkinson wrote that he was " imploied
in service upon the Seas against the Queenes enemies."

Now that his presence in Russia had become so necessary Elizabeth referred to him in a letter to Ivan as her
" orator and servant, dear to and beloved by us." He
will tell you, she continued in answer to the Czar's last
insulting letter, " that no merchants govern our country,
but we rule it ourselves, in manner befitting a Virgin
Queen, appointed by the great and good God."

When Jenkinson landed in Russia on July 26, 1571,
he found the country in a tragic condition. The break
in Anglo-Russian relations was a small matter compared
with the real disasters which had overtaken the empire.
The Krim Tartars had risen in revolt and sacked Moscow
itself. Famine and plague ruled the land. Some 300,000
persons had died of disease and starvation in the country
districts and another 300,000 in the burning of the capital.
Jenkinson saw people eating the bark off the trees and
heard tales of them eating each other.

Nor did he find his own position a very happy one.
The first thing he learned upon disembarking was that
Ivan was so enraged against the English that he had
promised to cut off his—Jenkinson's—head if he dared to
come to Moscow. He wrote that he was " not a little
dismayde " at the prospect of such a reception at Court
but that after reflecting upon his innocence he decided
to brave the anger of the Czar " notwithstanding his
tyranny." Jenkinson had never been the man to run
from danger.

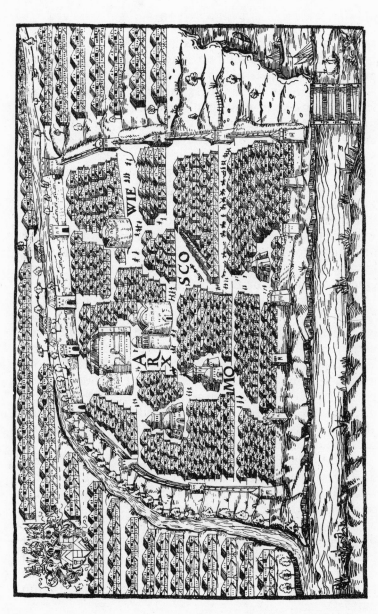

PLAN OF MOSCOW

From Sigismund von Herbertstein's "Rerum Moscoviticarum Commentarii," 1549

He made his way inland as best he could, although the refusal of the Czar to recognize his ambassadorial status subjected him to all manner of indignities on the road, and succeeded in reaching the town of Pereslavl where Ivan was then holding Court. For a time the Czar refused to receive him and, although he did not have him executed, kept him a prisoner.

At last he was admitted to formal audience. Jenkinson read the long oration which had been dictated by Elizabeth and the Czar listened gloomily. Then the Court was dismissed and in private conference Ivan aired his grievances against the treatment accorded him by the English Queen. Jenkinson loyally protested that Elizabeth had nothing but the most cordial feelings for Russia, pointed out the advantages which Russia as well as England gained from the Anglo-Russian trade, and pleaded eloquently for a resumption of friendly relations and the restoration of the Muscovy Company's privileges.

He made a deep impression upon the Czar. Ivan asked time to read Elizabeth's letters and to examine Jenkinson's request for a new trading charter. When the Englishman was dismissed a dinner was sent to his lodgings " with great store of drinkes of divers sortes." Things were looking up.

Yet it was almost two months before Jenkinson was admitted to a second interview. This was of crucial importance. Ivan appeared " apparelled most sumtuously, with a rich Crowne upon his head, garnished with many pretious stones " ; but, if the Englishman was at first fearful of what this formal display of the Czar's magnificence might portend, he was soon reassured by Ivan's friendly tone.

Most important, the Czar told Jenkinson that he had decided to set aside his " princely and secret affaires " and would not " ymportunate our Syster any further."

Consequently he was satisfied with Jenkinson's explanation of England's attitude on the other points at issue,
and promised to restore to the Muscovy Company all
its former privileges.

Jenkinson himself was once more back in Ivan's good
graces. He was permitted to kiss the royal hand and
to drink from the Czar's own cup. His tact and
diplomacy, his old friendship with Ivan, had won the
day.

' And if the Queene, our sister," Jenkinson reports
the Czar as saying to him, " had not sent thee, Anthony,
unto us at this present, God knoweth what we should
have done to the said merchants, or whether we would
have called backe our indignation."

Never had Jenkinson come back from one of his
journeys with a record of greater success than when he
returned to London on September 10, 1572. After
all, he had single-handed saved England's trade in
Muscovy. He had done his job well and was now
ready to retire.

In 1568 he had married Judith March, the daughter
of John March who was a member of the Muscovy
Company, and had purchased an estate at Sywell in
Northamptonshire. Here he settled down, and although
he continued to serve his Queen by helping to promote
the voyages of Martin Frobisher, who sought Cathay
by the north-west, and by acting as one of the commis-
sioners in certain negotiations with the King of Den-
mark regarding navigation rights beyond Norway, he
never again travelled very far afield.

His reputation in England as a pioneer of English
trade and as a learned geographer was widespread.
It had won him the unusual reward of a royal patent
granting him a coat of arms.

" Anthony Jenkinson, Citizen of London," read this

official document, " being one, who for the s'vice of
his prinnce, Weale of his countrey, and for knowledge
sake, one of the greatest Jewells gyven by god to man-
kynd, hath not fearyd to adventure and hazard his lyfe,
and to weare his body with long and paynfull traveyll
into dyvers and sundry contreys. . . . In consideracion
of which his said traveyll, tending always to the honor
of his prince & Countrey (a p'fect proof of his vertue
and prowesse) and for a perpetuall declaration of the
Worthynesse of the sayd Anthony Jenkinson, We, the
kings of Armes aforesayde . . . have assigned, gyven,
and graunted unto the sayde Anthony Jenkyson these
Armes and Creast followeng."

Some little time after he had retired to Sywell he
enumerated the countries he had visited during the
course of his life in an interesting letter to his friend,
Richard Hakluyt. They included Flanders, Germany,
France, Italy, Spain, Portugal, the Levant, Greece,
Turkey, Asia Minor, the Holy Land, Algiers, Tripoli,
Tunis, the Arctic regions, Russia, Central Asia and
Persia.

" And thus," he continued, " being wearie and growing
old, I am content to take my rest in mine owne house,
chiefly comforting my selfe in that my service hath bene
honourably accepted and rewarded of her Majesty and
the rest by whom I have been emploied."

Here we may leave him, for he continued to live in
the quiet he had so well earned for almost thirty years.
It was not until 1611 that Anthony Jenkinson set out
upon his last and greatest journey.

III

JAMES LANCASTER, *died* 1618.

" To any other course then I have determined (by God's helpe) I will not be drawn unto."

JAMES LANCASTER.

CHAPTER VIII

A CHALLENGE TO PORTUGAL

BY the end of the sixteenth century certain events had occurred which were to give an entirely new direction to the expansion of England's overseas commerce. Trade with Muscovy and the basin of the Caspian continued, but the development of Elizabethan sea power opened a new route to the distant East. The seamen of England were able to give up that dangerous and futile attempt to find a northern passage to Cathay and instead follow the Portuguese trail around the Cape of Good Hope to the Indies and the Spice Islands.

The venture which laid the foundations for this trade was sent out in 1601 under the command of James Lancaster. But before tracing its course we must gather up the threads of English activity on the sea during the period which intervened between the inauguration of the commerce in Muscovy under Chancellor and Jenkinson and the first voyage of the East India Company. During this quarter century, Frobisher and Davis sailed to the north-west in search of a passage to Cathay ; a new expedition to the north-east was sent out under Pet and Jackman ; Drake braved the ships of Portugal and Spain to follow Magellan's path round the world, and Cavendish, Fenton, Wood, and Lancaster himself sailed the southern route with varying success.

There had been tremendous excitement in London after Frobisher's return from his western voyage in

1576. Not only did he bring back news of the passage to Cathay " which he doubted nothing to find and pass through," and an Esquimaux whom he had " plucked with main force . . . into his barque," but a sample of gold which he had found on the shores of Frobisher Sound. The merchants of London believed they saw the dramatic realization of their wildest dreams—trade with Cathay and gold which would put to shame the Spanish mines of Mexico and Peru. The Cathay Company was immediately formed, thousands of pounds invested by merchants and common folk, and a fleet of eleven vessels despatched to the new El Dorado. After a hazardous voyage, during which the fleet came so near disaster that Frobisher at one time resolved to blow up his ship and " with this peal of ordnance to receive an honorable knell," the expedition returned with the vessels laden with several tons of ore.

Excitement again spread throughout London. Never had hopes of easy wealth taken such hold upon the merchants. Then suddenly these high hopes collapsed like a pricked balloon. Panic succeeded to dreams of untold riches when it was learned that the state assayers had found so little gold in these tons of ore that two hundred weight yielded less than a pin's head of the precious metal, a tiny particle which the assayers obligingly fastened to their report with sealing-wax.

Yet even this tragedy did not discourage those seeking Cathay, nor altogether destroy England's confidence that some day its rich shores would be discovered. When Pet and Jackman sailed to the north-east, Hakluyt went so far as to give them precise directions as to just what they should do when they reached the empire of the Great Khan. He suggested " banketting on shipboord persons of credite " but only after perfumes had been placed beneath the hatches " to make ye place sweet against their comming aboord." Needless to

SIXTEENTH CENTURY MAP SHOWING NORTH-EAST AND NORTH-WEST PASSAGES

From Theatrum Orbis Terrarum of Abraham Ortelius, 1573

say the voyagers never had the opportunity to welcome the officials of Cathay with such delicate attentions, for their ships were blocked, as had been those of all their predecessors, by the icy barriers of the " north-east frostie sea."

John Davis also sailed confidently for the East, choosing the Western route in the firm belief that the passage to Cathay was " a matter nothing doubtful." But his failure served to cap the climax and at last England began to give up all hope of finding the East by other routes than those pre-empted by Spain and Portugal. Fortunately other developments had given rise to the belief that these southern passages by the Cape of Good Hope and Cape Horn might not remain for ever the monopolies of the Catholic powers.

The growing enmity between Spain and England had changed England's attitude from respect for Spanish rights to open challenge. Elizabeth spoke scornfully of the Papal Bull dividing the unknown world between Spain and Portugal as " the donation of the Bishop of Rome to his favorites " and was soon to declare that the " sea and air are common to all men." She encouraged Francis Drake in his piratical forays and when the " Golden Hind " returned from its circumnavigation of the world its commander's defiance of Spain won him the reward of knighthood. The Elizabethan seadogs were now unleashed and the booty they seized from the treasure galleons of Spain and Portugal ran into the coffers of England.

Attempting to reach the sources of this wealth rather than waylay it on its homeward route, Fenton got no further than Brazil, but Cavendish buccaneered his way around the world to spread terror among the Portuguese seamen in the waters of the Indian Ocean itself. Then came the defeat of the Spanish Armada and the legend of Spain's invincible sea power was for ever destroyed.

At last the way to the East was open to English seamen daring enough to attempt the southern passage.

The merchants of London were not slow to realize their opportunity. The trade from which they had been so long excluded now seemed possible and they became even more anxious to reach the Indies than the legendary land of Cathay. They knew for certain that those regions of the East discovered by Portugal were rich with the pepper and spices which London needed so badly. Had not the capture of the Spanish galleon the " San Felipe " yielded £100,000 of booty, and that of the " Madre de Deos " almost £150,000 ? If this was not enough, their ambitions had been stirred even more by the fantastic tales of Eastern wealth which had been brought home by Drake and Cavendish.

It is at this time, in 1591, that James Lancaster comes upon the scene for the first time. In the expedition which a group of merchants sent out under the command of George Raymond to establish a direct trade between England and the Spice Islands, he sailed as second-in-command.

We know little more of Lancaster's early life than we do of that of either Chancellor or Jenkinson. According to his own vague account he gained his first experience in trade among the Portuguese. He tells us that he " Lived among them as a gentleman, served with them as a souldier, and lived among them as a merchant." But the sole result of this early association seems to have been a deep and abiding hatred for the Portuguese and all their ways. It was one of the most pronounced traits in his character and we shall later find him refusing to treat with them because " faith and trueth they have none, neither will use any, unless it be to their owne advantage." For whatever real or imagined wrongs they may have done him, Lancaster was to take his revenge time and again.

Some time before open warfare had broken out between England and the combined kingdoms of Spain and Portugal, he had returned home. He commanded the " Edward Bonaventure "—a 300-ton merchantman which may have been named after Chancellor's " Edward Bonaventure "—in the fleet which was marshalled under Drake and Howard to repel the Armada, and it was in this same vessel that he was commissioned to sail to the East with Raymond.

The voyage of 1591 was not destined to found England's Eastern trade, although it helped to blaze the trail. Three ships sailed from London, but after being becalmed for a month in the " doldrums " one of them was forced to turn back because so many of its crew were stricken with scurvy. Then off Cape Corrientes the depleted fleet met fierce storms and a second vessel sank with all hands. The " Edward Bonaventure " was alone. But, as Chancellor had done under very similar circumstances, Lancaster pushed on towards the East. He had no idea of turning back. To give up before they had dared everything to reach their goal was an idea which seems never to have occurred to these English seamen of the sixteenth century.

Lancaster rounded the Cape of Good Hope, crossed the Indian Ocean, and touched at Penang and Malacca. But he did not feel that it was possible to attempt to open up trade with the natives. His crew was too shorthanded—thirty men had been killed in a fight with natives of the African coast, four had been struck by lightning, their " neckes being wrung in sonder without speaking any word." Also it was evident the survivors were too enfeebled by fever and scurvy to risk a long stay in the tropics. Better than submission to the delays and vexations of trade under these conditions, Lancaster thought the wise course was to return with his added knowledge of the East and seek to

6

reimburse the London merchants by capturing some Portuguese prizes.

After cruising about the Indian Ocean for some time and taking several Portuguese ships laden with pepper, the "Edward Bonaventure" was turned toward the west. Its crew demanded that they should return and Lancaster himself was so ill—at Ceylon he despaired of his life—that no other course was open to him.

The long voyage home was a succession of thrills : sea fights against the Portuguese, pirate attacks, and near shipwreck, while the crew at one time almost starved to death and at another threatened to mutiny. But the climax to these inconceivable adventures came when the "Edward Bonaventure," after rounding the Cape of Good Hope, found itself unable to cross the line because of contrary winds and with its "victuals now being utterly spent" was forced to head for the West Indies. They reached San Domingo and found provisions, started off again towards the north, and were swept back to the island of Mona. Here, while Lancaster and all of the crew were ashore except five men and a boy, the "Edward Bonaventure" snapped its moorings. Somehow or other the handful of seamen aboard her sailed the ship back to England ; Lancaster himself was picked up by a compassionate French captain and three years after he had sailed found himself once again in London.

This is, in brief, the story of England's first pioneering attempt to establish direct trade with the Indies. Only one of the three vessels which had set out reached its goal and it limped back to port with a half-spoiled cargo stolen from the Portuguese. Of the 198 men who had doubled the Cape of Good Hope only twenty-five returned. Yet the venture was far from being a complete failure. Lancaster had found his way to the Spice Islands and had challenged Portugal's control of the

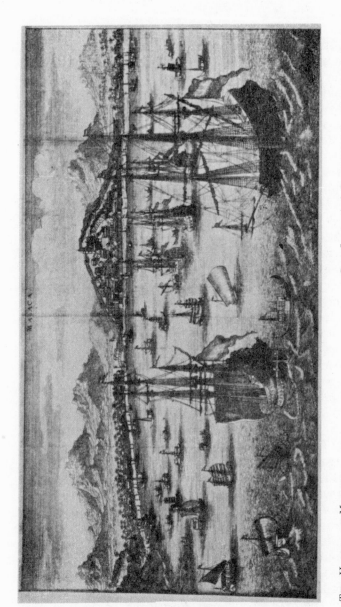

THE HARBOR OF MALACCA

From Constantin de Renneville's "Recueil des Voyages," 1725

Indian Ocean. He had attacked the galleons of his traditional enemies with impunity and seized their rich booty. As one historian wrote, his voyage " tore the Papal award of 1493 to shreds, and with it the charter of the Catholic monopoly in the Indian Seas." (9)

It would be natural to expect that Lancaster's report on conditions in the East would have resulted in the immediate launching of a second expedition, but some six years were to pass before this was done. Three vessels—the " Bear," the " Bear's Whelp " and the " Benjamin "—did set out under the command of Benjamin Wood with letters from Elizabeth to the Emperor of Cathay, but, with the exception of this expedition which was never heard from again, no English ships sailed for the Indies until the formation of the East India Company. It took Holland's success in trading with the East to spur the London merchants to new activity.

The Dutch had taken advantage of their war against Spain to challenge Catholic sea power in the East and showed more perseverance in following the trail Lancaster had pointed out than did his own countrymen. In 1597 Cornelius Houtman returned from an unbelievably successful voyage and was able to submit to his government a treaty signed by the King of Bantam. Five other expeditions left Holland the very next year ; by 1601 fifteen had been despatched.

Here was a friendly rival winning the trade which might have gone to England. It did London little good to learn that Portugal's monopoly was a thing of the past if a Dutch monopoly was to take its place. But what finally awoke the English merchants from their lethargy was a prosaic act which affected every English household. The merchants of Amsterdam raised the price of pepper from three shillings to eight shillings a pound.

Here at last was something which aroused England to a realization of what foreign control of the trade with the Spice Islands really meant. A meeting was held on September 22, 1599, and plans first laid for a company which was to become the greatest trading company the world has ever known, the Honourable East India Company.

For a year the merchants represented at this meeting worked over their plans and sought Elizabeth's permission to undertake the Eastern trade. For a time political questions, consequent upon Elizabeth's hope of making peace with Spain, caused the Queen to forbid any voyage to the East ; but when at last these negotiations broke down her hands were freed. On the last day of the year 1600 a charter was granted to 215 knights, aldermen and merchants headed by the Earl of Cumberland, incorporating them as the Company of Merchants of London Trading in the East Indies and granting them a monopoly of the Eastern trade " for the honour of our Nation, the welfare of the People, the Increase of our Navigation, and the Advancement of lawful Traffic to the benefit of our Commonwealth." (10)

A company of merchants supplied the backing, and the demand for cheaper pepper afforded the final incentive, for an undertaking which in the pursuit of peaceful trade and with no idea of conquest was directly to lead the way to England's establishment of her Eastern Empire.

Once granted their charter, the merchants lost no time in launching their expedition. The matter of chief importance was the selection of its commander. It was suggested by the Lord Chancellor that they should appoint to this post Sir Edward Michelborne, a courtier who had a *flair* for adventure and had himself applied for a patent to trade in the East. But the merchants of the East India Company were not courtiers. Despite the inclusion of certain knights and aldermen in their company, they were, for the most part, grocers, tailors, goldsmiths, drapers, haberdashers, " yremongers " and " skynners." They had no intention of entrusting their affairs to a man more at home at the levees of Elizabeth than at their own councils.   Nor did they wish to risk their investments in the hands of a man who would be inclined to turn aside from trade and commerce to seek glory or adventure.   They had the imagination to dream of winning the wealth of the Indies, these staid London merchants, but they were at the same time practical men of affairs.

Consequently they boldly asserted their independence. In the face of the persuasions of officialdom, they begged leave to " sort theire business with men of their own qualitye lest the suspicion of the employment of gentlemen being taken hold uppon by the generalitie do dryve a greate number of the Adventurers to withdraw their contributions."

Their own choice for a leader of their expedition was Lancaster. He was the most logical candidate in all of England to head a venture having as its goal the Indies and the Spice Islands.

We have already seen that he had practical experience in the East and knew the Indian Ocean and its ports as did no other Englishman.   And following his memorable voyage to Penang and Malacca, in fact within five months of his landing in London, he had been sent out on another venture.   This second expedition was towards the West and was frankly a punitive raid against the Portuguese city of Pernambuco on the Brazilian coast ; but it is worth noting for the light it throws upon Lancaster's character.

He was in command of three vessels and while crossing the Southern Atlantic one of them disappeared.   Believing that it had turned back towards England, the sailors

on the remaining two ships were afraid to go on with
their force so weakened and urged Lancaster to give up
the undertaking. He emphatically refused. He had
appointed a rendezvous in Brazil and was confident his
third ship would meet him there, but in any event he
would sail on despite all the Portuguese in the world
because " to any other course then I have determined.
(by God's helpe), I will not be drawen unto."

His daring had its reward. The third vessel did in
time rejoin the fleet and Lancaster landed his little force
at Pernambuco. So vigorously did he lead the assault
against the Portuguese defences that their frightened
soldiers " piked their ordnance so steepe downwards
with their mouths, that they shot all their shot in the
sand." Pernambuco was captured and the loot which
the English found passed all expectations. A great
carrack from the Indies had just arrived and, in addition
to the Brazil wood and camphor which they had hoped
to seize, there was piled on the wharves of the town this
vessel's precious cargo of calico, pepper, spices and
" divers other good things, to the great comfort of us
all." Lancaster was forced to charter three Dutch and
four French ships, which happened to come into the
harbour, to carry all this wealth back to London.

Frankly piratical as this expedition was, it served
to confirm Lancaster's courage and ability. It marked
him as a man specially equipped to run the gauntlet
of Portuguese ships in the Indian Ocean. Yet at the
same time Lancaster was primarily a trader and could be
counted upon not to lose sight of the chief aim of any
voyage to the Indies by giving way to the temptation
to become an open buccaneer. He had consistently
urged the opening of trade relations with the Spice
Islands throughout the period following his return
from the East. He had taken part in the early meetings
of the merchants who formed the East India Company

and was one of their twenty-four " committees." In
short, he was a man " of their own qualitye " and at the
same time an experienced and daring seaman with a
first-hand knowledge of the Indies.

Queen Elizabeth readily confirmed the Company's
appointment of such a likely candidate to head its first
voyage. He was given a " commission of martiall
law " granting him full authority over his seamen and
furnished with six letters to those Eastern princes with
whom he might come in contact, letters which in their
vague generalizations much resembled those which
King Edward had addressed to " all Kings, Princes,
Rulers, Judges and Governours of the earth." In this
case they were addressed in blank :

" Elizabeth by the Grace of God, Queene of England,
France and Ireland (Defendresse of the Christian Faith
and Religion), to the great and mightie Kinge of ——,
our Loving Brother, greeting."

The vice-admiral of the voyage was John Middleton ;
the pilot-major, John Davis. The latter, who is of
course best known for his explorations along the north-
west coast of America, had also sailed to the Indies as a
pilot in Holland's second expedition under Cornelius
Houtman and had brought back a collection of Sumatran
coins to the Earl of Essex.

Four ships were carefully selected by the East India
Company to make up its fleet. The " Malice Scourge,"
a 600-ton vessel built for raids against the Spanish, with
elaborately carved bow, great high stern, and carrying
ten pieces of ordnance, was bought from the Earl of
Cumberland. It was renamed the " Red Dragon " as
more appropriate for the " admirall " of a peaceful
trading venture, but its guns were not dismantled. It
carried a crew of 202 men. The other ships were the
" Hector," 300 tons and 108 men ; the " Ascension,"
260 tons and 82 men, and the " Susan," 240 tons and

88 EASTWARD HO!

88 men. A pinnace, called the " Guest," was later
added as " victualler."

The four vessels were carefully fitted out for a twenty
months' voyage with provisions of bread, meal, meat,
cheese, butter, raisins, prunes, currants, beer, cider and
wine. Their cargo, chosen by the merchants upon the
advice of those who best knew the markets of the East,
was made up of iron, tin, lead, eighty pieces of broad-
cloth, eighty pieces of Devonshire kerseys, one hundred
pieces of Norwich stuffs, and a large amount of Spanish
gold. In all some £72,000 was invested in the expedition.

Lancaster was instructed to seek agreements for free
trade among the island kingdoms of the East Indies
and to exchange his cargo at the greatest possible
profit for pepper and spices, with the purchase of small
quantities of such products as musk, ambergris, wax,
camphor, opium, silk and precious stones.

When at last all these preparations were completed
the committees of the East India Company gathered
at Woolwich on February 13, 1601, to bid God-speed
to this fleet which bore the hopes of all England for a
new and profitable trade with the Spicerie. It was a
memorable day in the history of England. No expedition headed towards the East had ever left its shores
destined to play such an important rôle in the development of the British Empire.

As Lancaster gave the signal to weigh anchor and
the seamen hoisted the great sails a cheer ran through the
crowd assembled on the banks of the river. There was
a shouting of farewells and, with flags and pennants
fluttering in the breeze, the four vessels and the little
pinnace slowly got under way and sailed down the
Thames.

CHAPTER IX

THE RICH AND GOULDEN ISLAND

SEVEN long and weary months were spent in the Southern Atlantic before the fleet reached even the Cape of Good Hope. They were driven off their course by contrary winds and perilously becalmed in the doldrums, just as Lancaster had been on his first voyage. Their fresh supplies ran out and, with scurvy—a scourge more dreaded by the seamen of that day than either shipwreck or enemy attacks—stalking through the forecastle, the men sickened until they could scarcely man the ships. Once they sighted and captured a Portuguese carrack, helping themselves to a cargo which included 146 butts of wine—" which was a great help to us in the whole voyage after "—but despite this lucky addition to their larder the scurvy continued to claim its victims. When the anchors were finally dropped at Table Bay, 105 men of the crews of the " Hector," the " Ascension " and the " Susan " had died.

Fortunately there was a different story to tell of the health of the men on the " Red Dragon." Few of Lancaster's own crew had fallen ill because their commander had " brought to sea with him certaine bottles of the juice of limons, which he gave to each one as long as it would last, three spoonfuls every morning fasting, not suffering them to eate anything after it till noone." He knew too well the toll scurvy exacted and somewhere in the course of his travels he had heard of this remedy. [11]

But for the sake of the men on the other vessels Lancaster was forced to decree a long rest at Table Bay. Tents were pitched on the shore and in exchange for pieces of old iron hoops the men bartered for beef and mutton from the natives. One thousand sheep and forty-two oxen were bought : the prices were one piece of iron eight inches long for a sheep, and two pieces for an ox. Fierce as he might be against the Portuguese, Lancaster had a friendly way with these natives. He talked to them, says the chronicler of the voyage whose fascinating narrative may be found in " Purchas His Pilgrimes," in " cattels language " which had not been changed " at the confusion of Babell." By means of gestures and the use of " ' moath ' for oxen and kine, and ' baa ' for sheepe " he made himself easily understood.

When the men had fully recovered, the four ships set out again toward the East. They sailed leisurely over the torrid waters of the Indian Ocean, landing at several islands in their course. But on one halt thirteen men died from drinking impure water and when the captain and boatswain mate went ashore for their burial, a salute was fired which unhappily struck the landing boat. Both men were killed " so that they that went to see the buriall of another, were both buried themselves."

At another island where " there came from the land such a pleasant smell, as if it had been a garden of flowers," the mariners had a more fortunate experience. Friendly natives sold them " hennes and Coco Nuts " and they found the waterfowl so plentiful that they could kill them with their oars. The result was that they enjoyed the best dinner they had had since leaving England.

It was more than a year after they had first set sail that they drew near to the island of Sumatra, and on

June 5, 1602, anchored off Achin, a port on its northern coast.

This was their first objective. To us nothing but an obscure Dutch province, Achin was a logical goal for these merchant adventurers. At the opening of the seventeenth century it was an important centre for Eastern trade. It lay on the highway to the Spice Islands, to China, and to Japan. For a time there was no more flourishing port in the Indies. Ships from as far east as the Moluccas and as far west as Arabia had long since sought its commerce. Arab and Chinese traders, Indian junks from Pegu, Gujerat and Bengal, were as familiar to the people of Achin as their own native craft.

Sumatra itself, the "rich and goulden island," was said by legend to be that Ophir where the fleets of Solomon had sought their gold. It now produced not only the much desired pepper, but offered to the traders of the Orient rubies and sapphires, camphor and wax, "gummes, balmes, drugges and Indico." It was a rich storehouse of the products of the East. "The Ile Sumatra," wrote John Davis, "is a pleasing and fertile Soyle . . . the whole Countrey seemeth to be a Garden of pleasure."

Marco Polo had paid the island a brief visit in the thirteenth century with the Chinese fleet which was carrying to her new home the beautiful Cathayan bride of the King of Persia, but the first European vessels to touch its shores were those of Portugal. They had landed at Achin in 1508. Its proud and haughty ruler had not submitted to Portuguese domination as had so many lords of the eastern isles. He had bitterly resented their intrusions and attempts to subjugate an empire which included all of northern Sumatra, with a coast-line of a thousand miles, the adjacent island of Nias, and the Malay states of Johore, Pahang, Perak and

Kedah.   He had warred steadily and successfully against
their settlement at Malacca.

The people of Achin were distinct from the other
races of Malay blood.   Tall and dark-hued, they claimed
descent from the Arab traders who had brought Islam
to the peoples of Malaysia in the thirteenth century.
They were fierce and brave fighters but also indolent
and shiftless.   The hot, damp climate of Sumatra was
not productive of energy and their life degenerated into
a matter of eating and watching cockfights.   The
products so highly prized by the Europeans were
cultivated with lazy carelessness and a primitive community raised its chief crop of rice by ploughing the
rich ground " with small skill and less diligence."
The English found the Achinese " inhumayne and base,
and much unworthie to inhabite so sweet a countree."

When Lancaster reached this port he found its
roadstead crowded with " eighteene saile of shippes."
Junks from all over the East were there with cargoes of
pepper, spice and silks, while sampans and native proas
darted in and out among the vessels lying at anchor.
The Achinese fishing-craft returning from the open
waters made their way up the river to where the city
lay buried in a jungle of palms and bamboo trees.   The
King's navy of great gondola-like vessels with oarsmen
in their bamboo outrigging lay at anchor in the harbour.
The English were amazed at the size and apparent
seaworthiness of these galleys, which could carry four
hundred men ; they were even more surprised at the
skill with which the natives handled their tiny proas
and at the " verie exquisite " way they could swim
and dive.

The East India Company's fleet was soon overrun
with visitors and to Lancaster's great satisfaction it
developed that the Achinese knew very well who the
English were.   Two Dutch merchants—for Holland

Mr. John Nieuhoff's Remarkable VOYAGES & TRAVELLS into ye best Provinces of ye West and East Indies.
VOL. II.

A ROYAL ELEPHANT *From Churchill's "Voyages," 1744*

had already established a trading factory at Achin—
informed the English captain that the " Queene of
England was very famous in those parts, by reason of
the warres and great victories which she had gotten
against the King of Spaine." The Achinese ruler,
Lancaster was told, felt that his enmity against the
Portuguese and Spanish was a strong bond between
him and Elizabeth. [12] If the English had come to
his shores seeking peaceful trade, there were no
foreigners whom he would more gladly welcome.

This was an auspicious opening for England's trade
relations with the East and Lancaster promptly sent
ashore envoys to tell the King that he bore a letter for
His Majesty from the Queen of England. They returned reporting a cordial reception at Court and a
marvellous banquet in their honour for which the Achinese King had requested that Lancaster should land
and " have kind audience and franke leave, with as
great assurance as if he were in the kingdome of the
Queene his mistris."

Putting ashore the very next day with a company of
his men, Lancaster was met by the Achinese officials.
Six royal elephants, distinguished by their gold teeth,
had been sent by the King " with many trumpets, drums
and streamers, with much people, to accompany the
generall to the court." The largest of these elephants,
which was some thirteen or fourteen feet tall, had " a
small castle, like a coach upon his back " on which had
been placed a great gold basin covered with a piece of
richly embroidered silk. Here Queen Elizabeth's letter
was solemnly placed. Lancaster clambered on the
back of another of the elephants and with some of his
men mounted and some on foot, the strange procession
made its way past throngs of wondering natives to the
royal Court.

They passed through what was known as the city of

Achin. It was really little more than a camp pitched on the edge of a dense jungle which was continually encroaching upon its flimsy barriers. The rude huts of the natives, which the English found " the poorest and weakest things in the world," were perched precariously upon stilts some eight feet high to protect them from the floods of the rainy season and the wild animals which roamed through the settlement at night. Their walls and roofs were made of bamboo mats and the floors of rough wood. Grouped together in compounds, they were separated by thatched walls from the streets and market places which were overrun with pigs and mangy dogs.

The English visitors found that the King's palace, which was on the outskirts of the city, was no better than the other native houses except that it was somewhat larger and surrounded by palisades and ditches. Here the Achinese ruler waited with his Court for Elizabeth's envoy.

This petty sovereign, whose name was Ala-uddin Shah, was a despot who ruled tyrannically the people of Northern Sumatra and those parts of the Malay Peninsula which acknowledged his authority. He held his subjects little better than slaves. Born a fisherman he had won the throne by his sword and, on assuming power, had coolly executed a thousand of the Achinese nobles to make room for his own supporters. Burning in oil was a not uncommon fate for those who dared to question his power. A noble might be blinded for looking at one of his thirty concubines. A whole island off the Sumatran coast was inhabited by the poor wretches whose legs and arms he had had cut off for offending him.

In his younger days, for he was at this time more than ninety, he had waged incessant warfare against the Portuguese because they would not recognize his

authority on the Malay Peninsula and had raided their
settlements with impunity. Now he was too old and
indolent to go to war and his fleet of one hundred
galleys was commanded by a woman because he would
trust no man. " He doth onely spend the time," we
read in John Davis's description, " in eating with women,
and Cock-fighting." When he had finished one banquet
he would chew betel nut wrapped in a palm leaf until
" by this means getting againe his stomacke he goeth
with fresh courage to eating."

When Lancaster was ushered into the presence of
this Malayan prince he found himself in a large open
room whose matted walls were hung with velvet
tapestries and cloth of gold. There was no furniture
of any kind and the King sat cross-legged on a bare
mat—" like a Taylor." His person was gross and fat.
His robes were of rich silk and his turban gorgeously
bejewelled. In the folds of the gown from which his
bare feet and legs protruded so incongruously were
stuck four diamond-studded krisses, the short, jagged
daggers of the Malays. In his lap lay a long, gold
sword.

The King was surrounded by his women, some
forty of them. They fanned him, stood by with goblets
of aqua-vitæ and with " clothes to dry his sweat." He
was chewing betel nut and spat frequently into a golden
cup which one of his slaves held ready for him.

The English envoy made no sign that this barbaric
scene was in any way strange to him, but gravely saluted
His Highness in the Malayan fashion with hands above
the head, palms together. He bowed slightly and cere-
moniously presented the letter which he brought from
Queen Elizabeth. This document had been duly filled
in to address the " mightie Kinge of Achem, &c. in the
Island of Sumatra, our loving Brother, greeting," and
requested " lawful traffique of merchandizing " and a

" perpetuall confirmation of love betwixt our subjects
on both parts." A gentle reference to the Portuguese
who " pretend to be monarchs and absolute lords of
all these kingdomes and provinces, as appeareth by
their loftie title in their writings," was especially calculated to win the favour of this monarch who had so
vigorously given " warres unto the Portugals in the
lands which they possesse."

Naturally Ala-uddin Shah was deeply gratified at
such an address and told Lancaster that his Sovereign
was " worthy of all kindnesse and franke conditions,
being a princesse of great noblenesse, for fame speaketh
so much of her." Nor was his pleasure lessened by
the next feature of the audience—the presentation of
Elizabeth's gifts. A great silver basin with a fountain
inside it which weighed 205 ounces, a large silver cup,
a rich looking-glass, a headpiece with a plume of feathers,
a case of daggers, an embroidered belt, and a feather
fan constituted the English Queen's friendly tribute
to her loving brother of Achin. The King took the
fan himself and at once " caused one of his women to
fanne him therewithall, as a thing that most pleased him
of all the rest."

Lancaster then sat down before Ala-uddin Shah,
cross-legged on a mat, and the signal was given to serve
a banquet. A procession of slaves entered the room
bearing hundreds of tiny dishes of gold and silver which
were set on the floor before the King and his guests.
They were heaped with rice, meat, pastry and sweetmeats. Flagons of arrack were also served ; but in
the exchange of toasts Lancaster found the Malayan
spirits so strong that he " drancke either water mingled
therewithall, or pure water," begging the King to excuse
him for this breach of etiquette.

After this royal repast the King's dancing girls were
summoned, and while other women beat on little drums

and droned an endless story of the glorious conquests
of Ala-uddin Shah, these alluring maidens in spangled
costumes hung with jewels and little golden bells entertained the King's guests. The dance was one of mimic
love scenes and mimic battles, strange and disturbing.
The Achinese nobles sat about with eyes tightly shut,
for it was forbidden them to gaze upon the King's
women, but not so the English. They watched with
fascination this glamorous spectacle which was so
symbolic of what they had been led to expect in the
Courts of the Orient.

When the dancing girls had withdrawn and the
Achinese nobles were again able to open their eyes,
the King presented certain gifts to Lancaster—" a fine
white robe of calico, richly wrought with gold, and a
very faire girdle of Turkey worke, and two cresses."
He was asked to put on these gifts in the King's presence
and with his white Malayan gown flapping over his
doublet and hose, the krisses in his " faire girdle of
Turkey worke " clanking against his sword, Elizabeth's
envoy was " dismissed the court, with very great
curtesies."

Within a few days Lancaster again made occasion
to visit the King and this time brought up the matter
of the proposed treaty which would allow trade between
Achin and England. Ala-uddin Shah was more than
favourable to this proposition. He appointed two
nobles, one of them the " chiefe bishope of the realm,"
to draw up the necessary articles in conference with
the English.

At these meetings Lancaster skilfully advanced his
arguments in favour of a close relationship between the
two countries. England was prepared to offer Achin
protection against their common enemies, the Portuguese and Spanish, while the projected trade would
bring new profits to all of Sumatra. " The royaltie of

7

the kings crowne," he told the Achinese negotiators, "will greatly increase, to the decrease and diminishing of all the Portugals trade." Furthermore, in return for the privileges of free commerce Queen Elizabeth would send out artificers to teach the Achinese the crafts of England. "And any other necessarie that our countrie bringeth forth and may spare," Lancaster promised, "shall be at the king's command and service." His single stipulation was that such requests should not be contrary to the honour of Elizabeth or to the "laws and leagues she may hath made with all the Christian princes, her neighbors."

The treaty was drawn up without difficulty and in due course signed by the King. It provided among other things for complete freedom of trade without customs dues, for the sanctity of contracts made between English and Achinese subjects, for redress for any injuries done the English, for the right of the English to execute justice on their own men, and for liberty to worship according to the dictates of their conscience.

This "holie league" between Ala-uddin Shah, the mighty King of Achin, and "our well beloved the Serinissima Regina de Engla Terra," was the first treaty to be negotiated by the East India Company. Insignificant as it may seem when we consider the treaties which this company was later to sign with the princes of India, it was the first real bond between the British throne and a kingdom of the Far East. [13] It represented a forward step in the expansion of English commerce of which the ultimate results were as utterly inconceivable to the doughty English sea captain as they were to the petty Malayan prince who had fixed his signature to the pact.

But despite the conclusion of this agreement the merchants aboard the English vessels were finding the matter of trade more difficult than they had been led to expect. Not only was pepper far more expensive than they had been told it would be, but there was very little of it in the market. Lancaster became greatly worried over this phase of his task. " He daily grew full of thought how to lade his shippes to save his owne credit, the merchants estimation that set him aworke, and the reputation of his countrey ; considering what a foule blot it would be to them all in regard to the nations about us, seeing there were merchandise enough to be bought in the Indies, yet he should be likely to return home with empty ships."

Like all the early adventurers in the East, Lancaster was faced with two problems. As important to him as bringing home a full cargo which would reimburse the merchants who had invested in his voyage was the maintenance of the dignity and prestige of his country " in regard of the nations about us." He realized only too well that success in whatever he undertook was the only thing which could preserve England's great reputation.

It was partly this idea of proving the might of English sea power and partly a yielding to a temptation which he apparently could not long resist which were responsible for his next step. He decided that, while all the pepper available at Achin was being loaded on one of his ships, he would take the other three and practise his old art of preying upon the commerce of Portugal.

There was all the more reason for this move because he feared that unless he struck first the Portuguese might attack him. They had an ambassador at the Court of Ala-uddin Shah and through spies Lancaster had learned that this man, who " had a diligent eye over every steppe we trode," was planning to return to Malacca and marshal a force to dispel the English fleet before it succeeded any further in encroaching upon the Portuguese trade.

The English found a ready ally for their counter-plot in the Achinese King. His slumbering resentment against the Portuguese had but recently been fanned into new flames by their peremptory demand that they should be allowed to build a fort at Achin. At this very time he was negotiating with the King of Siam for a joint attack upon Malacca. Consequently he was only too glad to agree to Lancaster's suggestion that the Portuguese ambassador be detained long enough to enable the English to put to sea and intercept one of the enemy galleons. His only condition was that Lancaster should bring back with him a " faire Portugall maiden."

With three vessels the English captain then set out. After some days of cruising about the Straits of Malacca their quarry was sighted, a great galleon of 900 tons. The English ships quickly surrounded it and opened fire. For a time this huge, lumbering vessel put up a stiff resistance, but when the " Red Dragon " fired " six pieces together out of her prow " and the enemy's " maine yarde fell down," the brief naval engagement was over. Lancaster had his prize. Boarding her, he discovered that she carried 600 passengers and a rich cargo consigned from Bengal to Malacca.

With business-like efficiency the English set about transferring 950 packages of calico and pintado (painted cotton) to their own vessels. Remembering that all this booty was for the merchants of London, and that he was a trader and not a buccaneer, Lancaster took stringent measures to prevent any " rifling, theeving, pillaging, or spoiling." In five or six days the unfortunate galleon was emptied and, leaving her to seek a new cargo wherever she might, the English sailed back to Achin.

There was great rejoicing at the success of this venture both among the English and the Achinese. The old King was delighted and graciously consented to accept

The Taking of y^e City of COTCHIN in ...

NAVAL WARFARE IN THE INDIES

From Churchill's "Voyages"

some of the prize goods which Lancaster diplomatically offered him. He had not forgotten his " faire Portugall maiden " and asked the Englishman why she was not included among the spoils. Lancaster gravely answered that it was only because " there was none so worthy that merited to be so presented."

If the English captain had not already won the favour and confidence of Ala-uddin Shah, this exploit would have assured his popularity at the Achinese Court. The King had not forgotten his own adventurous youth and could not but admire the courage of a seaman who set out so debonairly on seas infested with Portuguese ships and returned with a rich prize captured from in front of their eyes. He found in Lancaster those courageous qualities which were the best points of Malay character, and also recognized that the Englishman's firm control over his seamen—whose fondness for arrack sometimes made them hard to handle—proved that he was a man born to command. Nor had Lancaster offended him by any of those insolent demands which he was accustomed to receive from the Portuguese. He had shown both tact and an understanding of the Malay character in all his dealings with the Court, and, while he had at all times upheld the majesty of Queen Elizabeth, he had flattered the Achinese monarch by treating him with the respect which was shown to him by his own subjects.

Ala-uddin Shah always made the Englishman welcome at the various ceremonies and entertainments of his Court. Without doubt Lancaster was permitted to see the royal bath when the King sat on a raft in the midst of the river and water was poured over him for five or six hours from golden goblets. This was a formal ceremony always followed by a banquet. The guests were compelled to sit in the water while Malay slaves swam out to them with the dishes and goblets of wine—"such plenty of hot drinkes, as might have sufficed a drunken army "—held high above their heads. (14)

Lancaster also accompanied the King on his triumphal processions about the city when he paraded in royal state before his cheering people with " musick plaieing before them alongst the streets " and companies of fencers fighting running duels in front of the royal elephants with swords and targets.   He watched the fights staged between wild animals : buffaloes so power-ful that sixty or eighty men could hardly pull them apart by the ropes attached to their hind legs, elephants which battled against a tiger tied to a stake, and rams which struggled against each other.   The elephants fought cruelly, we read, the rams fiercely ; but the " buffles most stomachfully."

One time the chronicler of Lancaster's voyage makes specific mention of the Englishman's presence at one of the King's favourite cock-fights.   This was the sport in which Ala-uddin Shah found the greatest pleasure. He always bet heavily but was not a good loser.   There is the story that he once bet on a large cock against a smaller one and was wild with rage when his cock was killed.   When he demanded some explanation of how this could have happened the frightened attendant could find no answer.   The King declared that it could only be due to failure to feed his cock properly, and callously ordered that the man responsible should have his right hand cut off.

We can imagine one of these occasions when Lancaster was present : the tall and dignified Englishman and the obese old King in his calico robe and jewelled turban squatting eagerly about the circle where two slaves hold the prized cocks with long, steel spurs attached to their legs.   They bet on their favourites.   Then suddenly the cocks are released and with a lightning-like flash of feathers they fly at each other and meet like two furies in mid-air. Perhaps one of the cruel spurs strikes home and the birds fall to the ground, a mass of tangled feathers. One of them limps away, dazed, and the other lies motionless where it has fallen. Ala-uddin Shah and Lancaster settle their bets, take a drink of the biting arrack, and lay their wagers for the next fight.

In this way Lancaster spent the time at Achin while the merchants in his company were arranging the cargoes on the English ships and taking on all the pepper they could buy. At last the time came for him to sail and he went to the royal palace for his last audience with the old King. As gifts for Elizabeth Ala-uddin Shah presented the Englishman with " three faire cloathes richly wrought with gold of very cunning worke, and a faire rubie in a ring," and for himself another ring with another great ruby. Then turning to Lancaster the King asked whether the English had with them the psalms of David. Not a little surprised, he answered that they had, and that they sang them daily.

" Then said the King : I and the rest of these nobles about me will sing a Psalme to God for your prosperitie, and so they did very solemnly. And after it was ended the king said : I would heare you sing another Psalme, although in your own language. So there being in the company some twelve of us, we sung another Psalme : and after the Psalme was ended the Generall tooke his leave of the king."

CHAPTER X

JAVA AND THE PASSAGE HOME

LEAVING Achin the English separated. One ship, now fully laden with pepper and cloth from the captured Portuguese carrack, headed directly for England; a second touched at another Sumatran port and then sailed for home with a cargo of pepper and cloves; while Lancaster went further east toward the island of Java with the " Red Dragon " and the " Hector."

The port they sought was Bantam, capital of the kingdom on the westernmost tip of the island which in those days held sway not only over western Java but over Borneo and parts of Sumatra. It had been visited by the Portuguese for the first time in 1511 and by the Dutch in 1596, when the former had been driven out and Holland established its first factory in the Indies. It was to prove a more profitable market than Achin. After Lancaster's voyage the English did not again touch at the Sumatran port until 1613, but they traded regularly with Bantam until the hostility of the Dutch forced them to retire and the city became the chief port for Holland's eastern trade.

At this time the Dutch were still friendly, and when Lancaster's two vessels came into the harbour, crowded with the varied shipping of the East, and " shot off a great peale of ordnance . . . such an one as had never beene rung there before," the English were welcomed both by their fellow Europeans and by the Bantamese.

The natives were much like the people of Sumatra,

though perhaps even more lazy and indolent. Bantam was a primitive community of frail bamboo huts, and like the Javanese of to-day the people simply wore " a tucke on their heads, and about their loynes a faire Pintadoe, all the rest of their bodies naked." The English found them to be " exceedingly proud, although extreame poore, by reason that not one amongst an hundred of them will worke."

The trade of Bantam, for it was the centre of a thriving commerce with China and the islands further to the east, was largely in the hands of Chinese. They controlled the market for pepper, cinnamon, cloves and the other spices with little regard for the Bantamese, and while they might " like Jews live crooching under them," they nevertheless robbed the natives of their wealth and sent it to China. These traders had settled in their own China-town, which was surrounded by a brick wall and had houses far more substantial than those of the natives. It was in their section of Bantam that the Dutch merchants had taken up residence and where the English were to establish their factory.

Lancaster's first task was to endeavour to open up relations with the Bantamese ruler who had at least nominal sovereignty over his once-powerful kingdom. Another of Queen Elizabeth's useful letters was hastily filled in with his names and titles, and after the usual exchange of courtesies the Englishman was received at Court. He found the King to be a boy of ten or eleven who greeted him graciously and accepted with childish pleasure the gifts which Lancaster presented in the name of Elizabeth. The matter of trade was taken up with one of the Bantamese nobles who acted as regent for the boy King, and without further parleys the English were told they might buy and sell freely and with as great an assurance of safety as though they had been in their own country.

They lost no time in going about their business. Within five weeks all that remained of the cargo they had brought from England was exchanged for 276 bags of pepper and the two ships were fully laden. Lancaster prepared to sail for England, first sending a pinnace on to the Moluccas to trade and settle a factory there against the return of the English ships in another year, and selecting three merchants and eight men of his company to remain for the same purpose in Bantam.

The instructions given to these merchants urged them to " agree together lovinglie like sober men " and to " meete together in the Mornings and evenings in prayer, [for] god whom yee serve shall the better blesse you in all your affaires." Lancaster was a faithful observer of those rules of piety which Sebastian Cabot had advanced fifty years earlier for the benefit of Willoughby and Chancellor. The East India Company had inherited all the traditions of those first voyages of discovery, and the stern note of religious faith runs through the whole story of its ventures to the Indies. Without faith in God and in an after-life Lancaster and his fellow seamen might never have risked their own lives so freely or sailed so adventurously on uncharted seas.

It was on February 20, 1603, two years after they had left England, that, having paid a final visit at Court and received a letter from the King of Bantam for Queen Elizabeth, the English started upon the long voyage home.

The calm and placid waters of the Indian Ocean enabled them to make an easy passage to the Cape of Good Hope, but in heading up into the South Atlantic a sudden storm broke with such fury that it " strooke a present feare into the hearts of all men." Then with their long voyage almost done, the ship laden with its precious cargo, the final goal almost achieved, the rudder

STORM AT SEA

From Johan Nieuhof's "Die Gesantschaft der Oot-Indischen
Geselschaft in dem Vereinigten Niederlanden," 1666

of the " Red Dragon " was torn off. Even the most experienced mariners could do nothing as the helpless ship " drove up and downe in the sea like a wracke, which way soever the wind carried her." They were swept southward into " hayle and snow, and sleetie cold weather," realizing that, unless the sea calmed and they could fashion a new rudder, they were lost.

Hope sprang up for a time when the ship's carpenter made something which they thought might serve to hold the ship to its course, but in the rough weather this improvised rudder was useless. The frightened seamen begged Lancaster to transfer them to the " Hector," which had faithfully followed her sister ship in its erratic course, but Lancaster refused to do so. True to the Elizabethan traditions of the sea, he would not abandon his vessel while it was still afloat.

" Wee will yet abide Gods leasure," he told his crew while the " Red Dragon " was buffeted by wind and wave, unable to make any headway as she wallowed in the overtowering seas, " to see what mercie he will shew us : for I despaire not to save our selves, the ship, and the goods, by one meanes or other, as God shall appoint us."

Yet he was none too confident in reality. He ordered the " Hector " to leave his own crippled vessel and make her way back to England. To her captain he entrusted a letter to the East India Company. " I cannot tell you where you should looke for me, if you send out any pinnace to seeke me," he wrote, " because I live at the devotion of the winds and seas. And thus fare you well, desiring God to send us a merrie meeting in this world, if it be his good will and pleasure."

There is the courage of the man, and his loyalty to the merchants who had entrusted him with the command of their venture.

Darkness now fell and for long hours the "Red Dragon" lay at the mercy of the sea. But as daylight flooded the eastern sky the storm died away as suddenly as it had first sprung up. The ocean was once again calm. And to the surprise and amazement of the "Red Dragon's" crew, there was the "Hector" still in sight. "These men regard no commission," grumbled Lancaster, but he must have been deeply moved by the loyalty of the comrade who refused to desert him. The captain of the "Hector," wrote one of the men on the "Red Dragon," "was an honest and a good man, and loved the generall well, and was loathe to leave him in so great distresse."

Another attempt was now made to repair the damage to the "Red Dragon," and the ship's carpenter made a new rudder out of the mizzenmast. Lancaster signalled for the "Hector," and the best swimmers and divers of the two ships went over the side to see if they could fasten it in place. It hung securely, and at last the seaman "had goode hope to obtaine one port or other to relieve ourselves withall."

Fortune smiled on them, and it was St. Helena which they managed to reach without further disaster. The two vessels were made shipshape and the men refreshed with the meat of the hogs and wild goats which overran the island. After a brief rest they set out again and on September 11, now two and a half years after leaving England, they "came to the Downes well and safe to an anchor."

The first voyage of the East India Company proved to be a great success. All four of the vessels returned with valuable cargoes, and the way to the East was open beyond any question of doubt. Lancaster was accorded a triumphal welcome. While the London merchants busied themselves with unloading the vessels,

so fearful of " rifling, theeving, pillaging, or spoiling "
that they provided for the porters " 6 sewtes of canves
doublett and hose without pocketts," he was fêted
throughout London. Elizabeth had died just a few
months before his return and James I was on the English
throne, but the new King was not slow to recognize
the significance of the voyage in which Elizabeth had
taken such an interest. Lancaster was summoned to
Court and knighted in honour of his services for English
trade.

Sir James never went to sea again. His health had
been worn down by his strenuous life in the unhealthy
climate of the Indies and he was now in a position to
retire. But this did not mean that he had outlived his
usefulness. His judgment and experience were of
immense value to his fellow directors on the board of the
East India Company, and for fifteen years his services
were at the disposal of those planning to sail to far-off
lands. . Not only was he active in promoting the
expeditions sent out by the company to the Indies, but
he inspired many voyages of discovery in other parts
of the world which he thought might lead to the greater
glory or profit of his country. There is one record of
this in the name given by William Baffin to a body of
water in the north-west corner of Baffin's Bay. It was
called " Sir James Lancaster, his Sound."

He died in May, 1618. The wealth he had acquired in
his trading with the Indies and as a member of the
East India Company went largely to charity, for he had
neither wife nor children. There is mention in his will
of one of his brothers and of nieces, nephews and cousins,
but the bulk of his property went to the Skynners'
Company and to one Mistress Thomasyne Owfeild,
widow, for distribution among the poor at her dis-
cretion.

Lancaster had the satisfaction of seeing the trade he

had initiated expand and become of ever-increasing importance, but he little realized the true significance of his memorable voyage. He still could not know that it was the first step in that expansion of English trade which was to lead to empire.

IV

WILLIAM ADAMS, 1554–1620

" Giving so admirable and affectionated commendatyons
of the Countreye as it is generally thought emongest us that
he is a naturalised Japanner."

JOHN SARIS, 1613

CHAPTER XI

THE WESTWARD VOYAGE

IN the story of England's gradual penetration of the Far East there is one chapter which stands by itself. It is that concerning the brief period during which trade relations existed between England and Japan and a friendly welcome was accorded to the merchants of the East India Company at the imperial Court of the Tokugawa Shoguns. It is a chapter dominated by the romantic figure of a Kentish seaman who was the first Englishman ever to visit Japan.

In 1566, when Elizabeth had been eight years on the throne and Anthony Jenkinson was setting out on his third trip to Muscovy, a twelve-year-old boy named William Adams started work as an apprentice in the shipyards of a certain Nicholas Diggins at Limehouse. With a new-found commerce with Russia and the ports of the Mediterranean, England had an ever-increasing demand for merchantmen. Her shipyards were humming with activity. The twelve-year-old boy, who had been born at Gillingham in Kent, one mile from Chatham, where Her Majesty's ships lay at anchor, early absorbed the active spirit which marked the age, and his experiences in the shipyard stirred his ambition to play a real part in England's struggle for new trade.

He listened eagerly to the tales told by his fellow workers of the wealth to be won in strange and distant places. He heard marvellous stories of the gold mines in Spanish America and of the Spice Islands which

Portugal still monopolized so arrogantly. It was inevitable that he should soon give up building ships to sail them.

By the time he was twenty-four we find him commissioned master and pilot in the growing navy of Queen Elizabeth with his own ship, the " Richard Duffield," a pinnace of 120 tons burden carrying a crew of seventy. When the shadow of the Spanish Armada fell over England the young captain took his orders from Drake and drove his vessel westward with supplies for the English fleet. Peace found him in the merchant service. For some eleven years he traded under the flag of the Worshipful Company of Barbary Merchants, a group which had been granted the monopoly of English trade along the Moroccan coast.

But Adams had dreamed of Cathay and Cipangu, India and the Spice Islands. He was no more able to resist the call of the East than had been either Jenkinson or James Lancaster. He decided he must sail to more distant ports than those of Africa.

It was still two years before the formation of the East India Company, and consequently his only chance to realize his ambitions was to take service with the Dutch. We have seen that after the successful voyage of Houtman, in 1597, the merchants of Holland immediately sent out five more expeditions. It was on one of these, following the example of John Davis, that Adams took service as pilot major of a fleet under the command of Jacques Mahu. He was desirous, as he later wrote, " to mak a littel experience of the small knowledg which God had geven me."

On June 24, 1598, he sailed from the Texel with five vessels : the " Faith," the " Hope," the " Charity," the " Good News " and the " Fidelity." Their aggregate tonnage was 735 tons and their crews totalled 491 seamen Their goal was the Spice Islands, but they were to

FRONTISPIECE AND TITLE PAGE OF "PURCHAS HIS PILGRIMES"

PVRCHAS

HIS
PILGRIMES.

IN FIVE BOOKES.

The first, Contayning the Voyages and Peregrinations made
by ancient Kings, *Patriarkes,* Apostles, *Philosophers, and*
others, to and thorow the remoter parts of the knowne World:
Enquiries also of Languages and Religions, especially of the
moderne diuersified Professions of
CHRISTIANITIE.

The second, *A Description of all the Circum-Nauigations*
of the GLOBE.

The third, Nauigations and Voyages of *English-men,* alongst the Coasts
of Africa, *to the Cape of* Good Hope, *and from thence to the* Red Sea,
the Abassine, *Arabian,* Persian, *Indian,* Shoares,
Continents, and Ilands.

The fourth, English *Voyages beyond the East* Indies, *to the Ilands of* Iapan,
China, Cauchinchina, the Philippina *with others, and the* Indian Nauigations
further prosecuted: *Their iust* Commerce, nobly vindicated against *Turkish*
Treacherie; victoriously defended against *Portugall* Hostilitie;
gloriously aduanced against Moorish *and* Ethnike *Perfidie* ;
hopefully recouering from *Dutch* Malignitie; iustly maintayned
against ignorant and malicious Calumnie.

The fifth, Nauigations, Voyages, Traffiques, Discoueries, of the *English* Nation
in the Easterne parts of the World: continuing the English-Indian *occurrents,*
and contayning the *English* Affaires with the *Great Samorine,* in the *Persian*
and Arabian Gulfes, and in other places of the Continent, and Ilands of and
beyond the *Indies*: the *Portugall* Attempts, and *Dutch* Disasters,
diuers Sea-fights with both; and many other remarkable
RELATIONS.

The First Part.

Unus Deus, Una Veritas.

LONDON
Printed by *William Stansby* for *Henrie Fetherstone,* and are to be sold at his shop in
Pauls Church-yard at the signe of the Rose.
1 6 2 5.

From Edition of 1625

seek the Indies not by the usual route about the Cape of Good Hope, but by Cape Horn. They were to follow the course first set by Magellan and then by Drake.

Some time later Adams was to describe this voyage, apologizing for his " stowtness," in letters addressed to his " unknown friends and countri-men " at the English factory at Bantam, and to the " loving wife " whom he had left in England. It is thus from his own account, as it appeared in " Purchas His Pilgrimes," that we draw the story of a voyage unparalleled in all the records of six-teenth-century travel. (15)

The fleet started off auspiciously enough, but when it approached the line the wind fell away and it found itself hopelessly becalmed. Supplies ran low and scurvy inevitably began to claim its victims. The men sickened and some few died. It became absolutely necessary to put into a port where they could get fresh provisions. Succeeding in time in reaching the coast of Guinea they landed near Cape Gonsalves, but even there few of the sick recovered, " having little or no refreshing, beinge an unhealthfull place." Finally at the island of Annobon they came upon a native settle-ment of eighty houses. They promptly attacked and captured it, making off with " oxen, oranges and divers fruits." The stricken sailors were somewhat revived, and turning westward the fleet headed across the South Atlantic.

They hoped to reach Cape Horn during the mild weather of the South American summer, but delayed by calm and then buffeted by contrary winds it was long past the favourable season before they struck the coast. It was, in fact, April, almost a year after sailing and with the Antarctic winter close upon them, when they first sighted land. Nevertheless they tried to make their way through the Straits of Magellan until icebergs and driving snowstorms forced them back to seek the protection of a harbour.

Of course their supplies were again giving out. The men were put upon a daily ration of a quarter of a pound of mouldy bread with a weak portion of mixed wine and water. "The scarcitie of victualls," wrote Adams, "brought such feeblenesse, that our men fell into so great a weaknesse and sicknesse for hunger, that they did eate the calves' skinnes wherewith our ropes were covered."

For six months, from April to September, they wintered under these horrible conditions on the bleak coast of Patagonia. "Raine, winde, snowe, hayle, hunger, losse of anchors, spoyles of ship and tackling, sickness, death, savages, want of store and store of wants," reads a Dutch account of this winter, "conspired a fulness of miseries. But especially the colde encreased their appetites and this decreased their provisions." The fleet lost by death one hundred men.

Adams chafed under this protracted delay. Careless of the dangers of attempting to round Cape Horn in winter he would have pushed ahead at any cost. But his urgings were overruled and he despondently recorded that "many times in the winter we had the winde good to goe through the straights, but our generall would not."

When spring did at last come they weighed anchor and rounded the Cape, only to find the Pacific even less kind to them than the Atlantic had been. For two months there was not a fair day to dry their sails and "the devil added mutinie in their miserable companie." Terrific storms rolled up out of the west, the worst they had yet encountered, and the tiny vessels were tossed about helplessly on mountainous waves. They were driven further and further south into the cold and ice from which they had just escaped. They lost all contact with each other, and when the weather at last cleared, the vessel on which Adams was serving as pilot, the " Charity," found itself alone on the broad expanse of the Southern Pacific.

This ship then worked its way slowly north to the coast of Chile, where a rendezvous had been appointed for the fleet to meet. Here for twenty-eight days it waited in the hope of sighting its companion vessels, but when they failed to appear it was forced to go on in search of provisions. Once again the sailors were gnawing at the leather-covered rigging.

They next dropped anchor near the island of Mocha, and were overjoyed when natives putting out to the ship in their canoes promised them wine, potatoes and fruits in exchange for iron and cloth. The captain of the " Charity " and twenty-three of his men confidently went ashore " meaning for marchandize to get victualls, having wonderfull hunger." But a thousand of the treacherous natives lay in ambush for the little party of twenty-four and " straight-way fell upon our men, and slew them all, among which was my brother Thomas Adams."

No worse tragedy could have befallen the " Charity." Separated from the other ships whose fate they had no way of knowing, its crew, half-starved and mutinous, had now lost their captain and almost half of the survivors of the voyage about the Cape. In this emergency we find Adams coming more and more to the fore. One Jacob Quackernaeck was selected to take the place of the murdered captain, but the English pilot became the acknowledged leader of what was left of the expedition which had set out from Holland a year and a half earlier.

He decided to sail northward along the Chilean coast, and near the island of Santa Maria, to their relief and astonishment, the crew of the " Charity " sighted the " Hope," one of the ships which they had by now given up for lost. But it too had met disaster. Its captain and

twenty-seven of its seamen had been slain, like the men of
the "Charity," in an attempt to procure supplies from
the natives.   The remnants of the two crews now joined
forces and sent out a land expedition to get by any means
possible the supplies which they had to find if they expected to survive.   Fortunately they came upon some
Spaniards, in Chile for trade with the natives, and seizing
them held them as hostages for a ransom of beef and
sheep.

The officers and merchants aboard the two ships now
held a council of war.   What should they do ?   The
obvious thing was to save the expedition from utter
disaster by seeking safety as best they could.   They were
in constant danger of shipwreck, of starvation should
their supplies run low and the natives again prove
treacherous, of capture by Spanish vessels, which would
not spare them for poaching upon Spanish territory.
Yet under these dire circumstances Adams reports that
the first problem these men considered was how they
" could make our voyage for the best profit of our
marchants."   Is it any wonder that when their seamen
were animated by such a spirit of loyalty that England
and Holland were able to break the Catholic monopoly
of the trade with the East ?

The decision finally reached was that they should
sail for Japan.   Not only did the Portuguese-infested
Indies now seem too dangerous, but another consideration was brought up which is illustrative of how great
the general ignorance of the East still was.   The ships
carried a cargo largely made up of woollen cloth, and
it was apparently only at this point that the merchants
in the expedition realized that " the most part of the
East Indies were hot countreyes " and that wool was
not the best product in the world to sell in the tropics.

Little was known about Japan.   Under the name of
Cipangu it had been one of the goals of eastern voyagers

ever since Marco Polo had written that the palaces of its kings were " covered with a plating of gold, in the same manner as we cover houses, or more properly churches, with lead." We have seen that England believed it to be the source of all the world's precious stones and spices. More recently the Spanish and Portuguese, who had been trading in its ports ever since its discovery by three Portuguese seamen shipwrecked there in a Chinese junk in 1542, had spread glowing tales of its fabulous wealth. No ships of either Holland or England had ever touched its shores, but there was aboard the " Charity " a Dutch seaman—one Derrick Gerritson— who had once been there on a Portuguese vessel. He assured the council of merchants and ships' officers that in Japan they would find a ready market for their woollens.

The decision once made, the two ships headed north. High seas and heavy gales still dogged them—" as wondrous storme of wind," wrote Adams, " as ever I was in." And wondrous it must have been, for it spelled the fate of the " Hope." On February 24 it disappeared in that tempestuous sea, never to be heard from again. Only the " Charity " was left to continue the voyage. [16]

This single surviving vessel of the five which had sailed from the Texel was battered and storm-wracked. There were but twenty-eight survivors of its original crew of 110. " Great was the misierie we were in," Adams wrote, " having no more but nine or tenne able men to go or creepe upon their knees ; our capitaine, and all the rest, looking every houre to die."

Yet they sailed on. Somehow during these last weeks Adams kept the " Charity " to her course and sailed her steadily toward Japan, inspiring the crippled crew to the best they could. How he did so passes all understanding ; but at length, when only five or six men were still on their feet, land was sighted. They drew near the island of Kyushu, and on April 19, 1600, almost twenty-two months after the day they had sailed so gaily from Holland, this lone vessel dropped anchor " about a league from a place called Bungo."

CHAPTER XII

COUNCILLOR OF IYEYASU

AS the enfeebled seamen of the "Charity" gazed wearily upon the shore of Japan, a host of native junks and sampans surrounded their vessel. The ship with its starving crew had crept into harbour like a ghost from another world, and the Japanese fishermen and sailors swarmed aboard to find out if this startling apparition were real. What they found evidently frightened them even more than had the "Charity's" first appearance. They quickly scuttled back to shore, stopping only long enough to pick up as souvenirs every removable object on the ship on which they could lay their hands.

Fortunately for Adams and his Dutch companions the feudal chieftain to whom they reported the vessel's arrival had had some experience wth foreigners. The Portuguese had traded under his protection in Bungo for many years, and the Jesuit missionaries, who had followed the traders, had made thousands of converts among his people. He had even sent a mission to Europe, for it was from Bungo that four Japanese noblemen had set out in 1583 to pay a memorable visit to the Pope and Philip II. Consequently the fears of the local populace were soon dispelled when they came to realize that this was but another of the foreigner's vessels. The daimyo sent word that the new-comers were welcome. The "Charity" was towed into safe anchorage, a house ashore was placed at the disposal

of the crew, and they were plentifully supplied with the
fresh provisions which they needed so badly.

As the vessel was neither Spanish nor Portuguese, it
still presented a difficult problem, however, and messengers were immediately sent off to seek instructions from
the feudal chieftain of all Japan, the great Iyeyasu, as
to what should be done.   While waiting word from the
Shogun the daimyo and his officials continued their
friendly hospitality, until an unexpected factor entered
the situation with the visit of some Portuguese Jesuits.
The priests did not welcome their fellow Europeans.
They saw in the Dutch sailors and their English leader
heretics and trade rivals.   They felt the danger to their
own position in Japan if these men were received in
favour, and the end of their monopoly should the new-
comers be allowed to trade.

They took prompt and energetic action to protect
themselves. The daimyo of Bungo was told that there
was something sinister about this mysterious ship.
Rumours began to spread through the countryside that
its crew were not seeking trade, but that they were
pirates.   Wherever the Jesuits went an ugly feeling of
suspicion and distrust sprang up. Adams and his
companions feared for a time that crucifixion, the fate
the Japanese meted out to all thieves and pirates, might
be the final end of their adventures.

But before matters came to a head word was received
from Iyeyasu. He ordered Adams to come to his
Court at Osaka.   Taking one Dutch sailor as his companion, the Englishman set out in a royal junk which
the Shogun had provided for him.

Their way led them through the Inland Sea.   They
skirted hundreds of tiny islands, sped by fishing-fleets
with their coloured sails reflecting the sunlight, passed
innumerable little villages whose thatched houses crowded
down to the shore, and so made their way to the mouth

INLAND SEA

From Arnoldus Montanus' "Ambassades Memorable . . . . vers les Empereurs du Japon," 1680

of the river leading to Osaka.   There Adams was met
by the emissaries of Iyeyasu and taken to the city, a
thick cluster of small wooden buildings spreading out
for miles over the countryside.   It was a city, we read,
as large as London.   Its narrow streets, running off
at right angles to each other, were crowded with artisans
and merchants.   Its shops differed little from those of
Europe.

Adams soon realized that this country he was visiting
was as civilized as the England of Elizabeth.   " The
people of the Island of Japon are good of nature, courte-
ous above measure, and valiant in warre," he was later
to report.   " Their iustice is severely executed without
any partialitie upon transgressors of the law.   They
are governed in great civilities.   I meane, not a land
better governed in the world by civil policie."

He was entirely right.   Japan at the opening of the
seventeenth century had embarked upon an era of peace
and prosperity which was to bring her civilization to
its finest flowering.   In many respects the Englishmen of
that day were barbarians in comparison with the orderly
and cultured people of this little-known land.   The
traditions of courtesy and chivalry, bravery and un-
faltering loyalty, which governed those of the samurai
class are too well known to need comment.

The man who was most responsible for the great age
of Japanese civilization was the powerful Shogun to
whose Court Adams was being conducted.   Iyeyasu
was the third of that triumvirate of Japanese soldiers
and statesmen which rescued the country from anarchy.
Nobunaga and Hideyoshi were the great captains
whose military exploits had done so much to unite Japan;
but it was Iyeyasu who completed their task and had
the statesmanship to establish the government upon a
firm and enduring basis.   Within a few months of
Adams' arrival he was to fight a decisive battle against

his enemies at Sekigahara, and after that victory, with
the single exception of the siege of Osaka in 1615, Japan
was to enjoy uninterrupted peace for two hundred and
fifty years under the dynasty he founded. The rule he
established was to last until the "black ships" of
Commodore Perry anchored in the Bay of Yedo and
foreign influence quickened the revolt against the
Shoguns that led to the restoration of the Mikado.

Like his predecessors, Iyeyasu arrogated all power unto
himself, and the shadowy figure of the legitimate emperor
reigned only over the descendants of the old nobility
at the phantom Court at Kyoto. Foreign visitors
recognized his religious significance as a descendant of
the gods and called him the pope, but to Iyeyasu, the
Shogun, they unhesitatingly gave the title of Emperor.

What manner of man was this who not only established peace in Japan but placed it upon such enduring
foundations ? Iyeyasu, above all else, was tolerant and
broad-minded in an age not conspicuous for these
qualities. A soldier, a law-maker, a diplomat, Lafcadio
Hearn declares that "he was one of the shrewdest,
and also one of the most humane statesmen that ever
lived . . . by the range and versatility of his genius he
might be not unfavourably contrasted with Julius
Cæsar." [17]   He was the most remarkable man Japan
ever produced.

The palace of Iyeyasu lay some little distance outside
the city of Osaka. It was surrounded by three thick
walls of stone separated by moats, and its approaches
were heavily guarded by soldiers armed with pikes,
swords, and bows and arrows. A few pieces of
foreign ordnance showed the influence of the Portuguese
traders. In the antechamber to the Court itself Adams
was kept waiting some time. There was a constant
coming and going of feudal chiefs bringing tributary
gifts to their leader and paying the visits to his Court

which he required as one means of preventing plots
against his rule. The daimyos and samurai, in their
silken gowns, accompanied by liveried attendants,
crowded past the strange and incongruous figure of
the English sailor, bronzed and weather-beaten from a
voyage of two years. The Japanese guards, in black
silk gowns and wide breeches, with the two swords of
the samurai stuck in their belts, must have regarded
him suspiciously.

When Adams received his summons to come into the
Shogun's presence he entered a "wonderfull costly
house guilded with gold in abundance." But it was
not a Court inviting comparison with the barbaric
splendour of that of Ivan the Terrible or those of the
Persian and Tartar princes whom Jenkinson had visited.
Its magnificence was subdued and restrained by an
appreciation of beauty as foreign to them as it would
have been to Elizabeth herself. Delicate sliding panels
took the place of walls and were covered with soft
paintings of Japanese landscapes. The beams and pillars
of the room were coated with gilt lacquer—the "gold
in abundance" which Adams described. There was
nothing on the highly polished floor but woven mats.

Iyeyasu sat in the shadows on a raised mat covered with
cloth of gold. His richly embroidered gown of silk
fell in graceful curves from his shoulders and in his
belt were swords of gold and silver. His head was
shaved to the crown, with a black top-knot. In his
hands he held a slender fan.

Adams answered boldly and without hesitation the
questions which Iyeyasu now put to him through a
Portuguese interpreter. The Shogun was curious and
interested in everything concerning his unexpected
visitor. Whence had he come, what were the character-
istics of his country, what was his purpose in travelling
so far, what was the nature of his religious beliefs?

Adams told Iyeyasu of the majesty of Queen Elizabeth, of the vigour and strength of England and its bitter antagonism to the Portuguese and Spanish, who confessed a religion which all good English Protestants held in abhorrence. He showed the Japanese statesmen a chart of the world to explain the long voyage he had just completed and declared that England sought peaceful trade, not conquest, throughout the world.

For Adams, we must remember, this was a crucial interview. The Jesuits had already carried to the Japanese Court their tale that the English were the " theeves and robbers of all nations," and they had the confidence of the Shogun. It was Adams' life which was at stake and the lives of his Dutch companions. There still hung over them all the dreadful shadow of crucifixion.

But none of the courage or self-respect of this Englishman deserted him because he was virtually suing for his life. He spoke no less boldly because he was in danger, and Iyeyasu was immediately impressed by his frankness and his blunt honesty. In his dealings with his own courtiers, or with the envoys of Spain and Portugal, the Japanese ruler had not been accustomed to such straightforwardness. " From one thing to another," Adams wrote, " I abode with him till midnight." And then, although he still did not know what his fate was to be, he could add, " He viewed me well, and seemed to be wonderful favourable."

After being dismissed he was held a virtual prisoner, but three days later there was another interview. Again Iyeyasu asked dozens of questions—about the countries of Europe and their wars, about their trade and products, about their livestock. He asked Adams of his belief in heaven. But still he did not give any decision as to what should be done with the new-comers and their inevitable request to be allowed to trade. When again dismissed, however, the English pilot's "lodgings were bettered in another place."

For forty-one days he was kept in suspense, looking every hour to die. The Portuguese were intriguing against him with every means at their disposal and trying to persuade Iyeyasu to execute all of the "Charity's" crew as enemies of Japan. It was a bitter duel in which Adams' only weapon was his own personality.

Fortunately Iyeyasu was a shrewd ruler. He knew the value of foreign trade and wished to encourage it. He realized that the desire of the Spanish and the Portuguese to retain their monopoly might have something to do with their bitter attacks upon the English and the Dutch. He saw no reason why he should become involved in the quarrels of Europeans who carried their enmities with them wherever they went. His fundamental policy was that of welcoming to Japan with equal hospitality all those who came seeking peaceful trade and agreed to abide by the laws of the country. Adams had convinced him that he came in peace, and so despite the protests of the Portuguese the decision he reached was to apply his rules of hospitality to the new-comers.

Adams was released. Yet so strong had been the impression he had made on Iyeyasu that while the Dutch sailors were recompensed for the goods they had lost and allowed to settle wherever they might please in Japan—not, however, being allowed to leave the country without permission—the pilot was to remain at Court.

So it was that this outspoken English seaman, rather than the wily Jesuits who had looked with jaundiced eyes upon all new-comers to Japan, became the medium through whom Iyeyasu learned of the Western world and maintained those slender ties which bound his empire to Europe. Adams' influence grew steadily, but, even more remarkable, there developed between the Englishman and the Japanese a friendship which was to endure until Iyeyasu's death.

All those foreigners who hoped to establish relations with the Shogun's Court soon began to realize that the Japanese ruler had to be approached through this Englishman who had won his favour and confidence. Adams was destined to remain on and on in a position of trust which makes the story of his life in Japan one of the strangest and most unusual in all the annals of the East. When another Dutch ship arrived in Japan some nine years after the " Charity " had dropped anchor at Bungo, it was Adams who secured for the merchants of Holland their trading privileges and persuaded Iyeyasu to grant the " Charity's " crew permission to return home. When the English eventually appeared upon the scene it was again Adams who introduced them at Court and induced Iyeyasu to grant the East India Company the most extensive privileges any foreign nation ever obtained. He even overlooked the intrigues of the Spanish and the Portuguese, and to their astonishment interceded for them at Court. And at the same time, in all his dealings with the merchants of these nations, attracted to Japan in the hope of exchanging their cargoes of " cloth, lead, elephants' teeth, damaske, black taffeties, raw silk and pepper " for gold and silver, Adams acted with an impartiality which proved his loyalty to Iyeyasu and to Japan.

On one important point in Japan's foreign policy he played an especially influential rôle. He readily welcomed traders ; but as a stout Protestant, scornful of the idolatrous ways of the Papists and believing simply in " God that made heaven and earth," he strongly opposed the entry into Japan of Catholic missionaries. He felt that the country was menaced, as he would have thought England menaced, by the activities of the

Portuguese Jesuits and Spanish Franciscans. They
brought with them the spirit of the Inquisition. They
persecuted those who refused to accept their religion and
stirred up their converts—who at one time numbered
more than 300,000—to violate and destroy the Buddhist
temples and the Shinto shrines. They were a source
of dissension and civil strife, a danger to Iyeyasu's rule.

The Jesuits and Franciscans knew his attitude on
religion and did their best to force him and the Dutch
to quit the country despite Iyeyasu's edict against it.
They feared the Protestants would " infect the Japanese
converts, tender in the Catholic faith, with their perverse
doctrines." But Adams could not be persuaded to try
to leave Japan, nor could he be induced to give up his
Protestantism when the priests tried to convert him.
It took an odd incident to convince these evangelists
that they were wasting their time with an " obstinate
heretic."

A Franciscan friar in mistaken zeal decided to prove
to Adams that miracles were still possible to those with
true faith. He would walk upon the water. On the
shore off the town of Uraga a great crowd gathered to
witness this proof of supernatural power. Adams and
the Dutch sailors, coldly sceptical, and throngs of
curious Japanese, watched the confident friar tuck up
his robes and with a great wooden cross in his arms step
off into the sea. Fortunately a small boat was handy for
his rescue. The experiment did little good for the
Catholic cause and the poor friar was indignantly recalled
by the authorities of his Church.

Adams' feeling about Catholicism was so strong that
he sincerely believed that under the cloak of religion
the priests were the forerunners of a military attack
upon Japan by the Catholic powers. And he did not
hesitate to impress his views upon Iyeyasu. The
activities of Spain in Mexico and Peru gave colour to

9

his suspicions, but there was also evidence nearer home
of a nature which thoroughly aroused the Shogun.
Christian converts in various parts of the country had
mysteriously united in uprisings against their feudal
chiefs.   They were invariably to be found in the ranks
of Iyeyasu's enemies.

As we know, the subversive activities of the Jesuits,
their arrogance and intolerance, eventually called down
upon them the wrath of the Japanese rulers.   They
were persecuted and expelled, their religion was ruthlessly stamped out, and Japan closed to them.   Two of
the Catholic historians of early Japan, Charlevoix and
Pages, assign to Adams the chief responsibility for these
later developments, and while this is an exaggeration
there is no doubt but that all the weight of his unusual
influence with Iyeyasu was thrown against the priests
at a critical period in Japanese history. (18)

The rôle of the Kentish pilot, however, was not
confined to that of adviser on foreign affairs and religious
policy.   In the frequent interviews he now had with
Iyeyasu he became his instructor in all the ways of the
West.   Despite the many differences between the Shogun
and the seaman, all the evidence points to a remarkable
community of interests.   They met on terms of equality.
There were no barriers of racial prejudice, no condescen-
sion on the part of the Japanese ruler and no humility
on the part of the Englishman.

Adams taught the Shogun " some points of jeometry,
and understanding of the art of mathematicks, with
other things," and then won his eternal gratitude by
building two ships for him.   At first the Englishman
was very reluctant about these ships.   He told Iyeyasu
that " by my profession I am no shipwright " and that
he " had no knowledg thereof."   But the Shogun was
insistent.   Japan had a growing commerce with China,
Siam, Cochin China and Malaya, and he wanted to

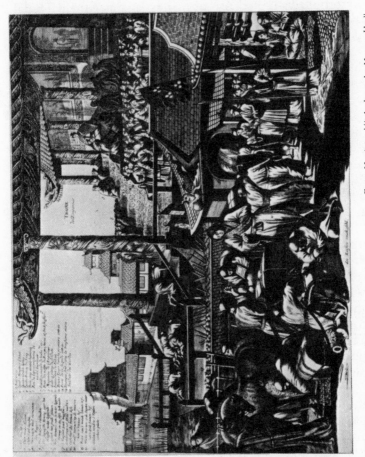

THE COURT OF THE SHOGUN

From Montanus' "Ambassades Memorables"

experiment with European vessels. If they did not turn
out too well, he told Adams, it would be " no matter,"
but European ships he must have.

The Englishman was persuaded, and having once
taken on the task set to work with characteristic energy.
He planned two pinnaces, one of 80 tons and one of
170, and ably directing the Japanese workmen whom
the Shogun had assigned to him soon had them afloat.
Iyeyasu was delighted. Nicholas Diggins, the shipwright of Limehouse, builded better than he knew when
so many years before he had taught a twelve-year-old
Kentish lad some knowledge of his trade. We may
consider the two vessels which his apprentice designed
for Iyeyasu as the direct ancestors of the Japanese navy.

There is no more conclusive proof of how greatly
Adams pleased Iyeyasu by these varied services than
the Shogun's continued refusal to allow the Englishman
to leave Japan. In 1605 Adams begged permission to
return to England, " desiring to see my poore wife and
children according to conscience and nature," but the
Japanese ruler did not take kindly to the idea. Adams
might write that " I please him so that what I said he
would not contrarie," yet on this point Iyeyasu was
firm. The Englishman's counsel was too valuable
for him to risk losing his services despite all Adams'
promises to return. The Shogun showed his favour
in many other ways ; but Adams wrote home that " by
no means he would let mee goe."

We are not wholly dependent on this evidence to
show the Englishman's position at the Japanese
Court, however. In the annual letter of the Jesuits
even his enemies are found reporting that he had obtained " such favour with this monarch that no lord or
prince of the land had better, because he had much
spirit, experience and sincerity. He often conversed
with the Emperor (the Shogun) and had ready access

to his presence, a favour which was accorded to few
people only." The other foreigners in Japan admitted
that he was in such favour " as never any Christian in
these parties of the world."

Iyeyasu himself showed the confidence in which he
held Adams by rewarding him with " a living, like unto
a lordship in England, with eightie or ninetie husband-
men, that be as my slaves or servants." He made him
a samurai and granted him a pension of two pounds of
rice daily and seventy ducats (about $150) a year.

His estate was at Hemi-Mura, eight miles from
Uraga, in a beautifully hilly region overlooking the
entrance to the bay of Yedo, where Perry's ships were
to anchor in 1853. Here the Englishman lived when
he was not at Court. There were upon his land
" 100 farms, or howsholds . . . besides others under
them, all which are his vassalls and he hath power of
lyfe and death over them as any tono (or king) hath
over his vassalls." In his dealings with these retainers,
Adams upheld all the traditions of the samurai class
to which he now belonged, and his serfs paid him in
turn the same loyalty which they would have paid to a
Japanese lord. When he returned home from his trips
to Court he was always warmly welcomed by his tenants
and neighbours. We can read in the descriptions of
later foreign visitors how his people would rush out to
greet him and escort him through the little villages on
his land to his own house, where his servants were
gathered bowing about the doorstep.

He lived as the Japanese lived, spoke their language
and wore their clothes. We must picture this rough,
broad-shouldered, fair-haired Anglo-Saxon dressed in
the silk robes of a Japanese courtier, his large, ungainly
feet in specially-made sandals, and in his belt the two
swords which were the insignia of his rank. He must
have made an unusual picture at the ceremonious Court

of Japan. What a strange thing for the Japanese to have this Elizabethan sailor who had become a samurai brushing past the daimyos and other feudal chiefs for his special audiences with their all-powerful Shogun. It is hard to conceive a more incongruous scene than Adams and Iyeyasu sitting cross-legged on their mats while the Englishman talked of the " art of mathematicks " or warned the Japanese ruler of Jesuit plots and the sinister purposes of Spain.

One other step Adams took which identified him even more closely with Japan. When he had about given up all hope of ever returning to England, he married a Japanese woman, and by her had two children to whom he gave the English names of Joseph and Susannah. There is no authentic record of the circumstances in which the wife he had left in England became, as he was to write, " in a manner a widdow," but this is the story which Japanese legend has preserved :

A beautiful Japanese girl was captured by bandits. Learning of her abduction Adams chivalrously attempted to rescue her, only to fall into the hands of the robber band himself. News of his favourite's brave but disastrous defence of the girl was brought to the great Iyeyasu, and the Shogun immediately came to his aid. With his own hand he slew the robbers and rescued the captive couple. Then to reward Adams, and also in the hope of persuading him to remain contentedly in Japan —there is a Japanese proverb that a woman's hair may bind even an elephant's foot—Iyeyasu gave him the girl in marriage. So Adams took her to Hemi-Mura and for ever after they lived happily in their home on the wooded hill overlooking the sea.(19)

Did Adams enjoy the strange life to which an uncertain fate seemed to have destined him ? We know that he tried to leave Japan and that he had pangs about his wife and children, whom he had left in England. In

one of his early letters which he despatched on a Dutch
ship, hoping it might fall into the hands of some country-
man, he begged whoever might receive it " in the name
of Jesus Christ to doe so much as to mak my being here
in Japon, knowen to my poor wife ; in a manner a
widdow, and my two children fatherlesse ; which thing
only is my greatest griefe of heart, and conscience."
Yet at the same time he most certainly did not spend
his time pining away in lonely exile.   He was too restless
and too active a man for that, and quite naturally adapted
himself to his new surroundings and to new circumstances.
He may have longed at times for England, as we know
he did, but he could never have settled down to a
prosaic existence in the quiet village life of Gillingham
or the shipyards of Limehouse.   The important rôle he
played in Japan must have largely compensated him for
his enforced exile.

He was not only a favourite at Court but known and
respected   throughout   the   country.   "I   am   called
Angin Samma," for so he put into English the Japanese
for " Mr. Pilot " in another of his letters, " and by
that nam am I knowen all the sea cost allonge."   No
foreigner,   with   the   possible   exception   of   Lafcadio
Hearn some three centuries later, has ever been identified
so closely with the life of Japan.   Yet, as we shall see,
he remained faithful to England.   He became a man of
two countries and of two loyalties.

While in England he is to-day honoured as the first
Englishman to visit Japan, in his adopted country there
are Japanese who trace their descent from " Angin
Samma," the favourite of Iyeyasu.   There is a street in
Tokyo which bears his name, and it is said that every
year the people of this street hold on June 15 a celebration in his honour.

CHAPTER XIII

THE ENGLISH FACTORY

IN 1613, after Adams had been thirteen years in Japan, there occurred a significant event which opened a new chapter in his life. An English ship, the " Clove," landed at the small island of Hirado on ˙he westernmost tip of Japan.

This vessel had been despatched under the command of Captain John Saris by the East India Company, whose commerce with the East had continued to expand after that first voyage undertaken by James Lancaster. The London merchants hoped that a new trade with Japan might be added to that already established with Achin and Bantam. Captain Saris brought with him a letter from King James to the Emperor of Japan, and as evidence that some of Adams' letters had reached home, instructions to get in touch at once with the English pilot.

Adams was at Court when the " Clove " arrived, however, and it was several days before the messengers despatched to inform him of the arrival of his fellow countrymen were able to reach him. In the meantime the new-comers waited at Hirado, and as soon as the daimyo of this island learned of their identity and that they bore letters to Angin Samma, he prepared to entertain them royally. With a troop of his retainers he came gaily aboard the " Clove," laden with welcoming gifts : venison, wild fowl, boar—" the largest and fattest that ever any of us had seene " —fruits, fish and " tubbes

of the Counterye wine." The ship was so overrun
with guests that Captain Saris wrote they " were not able
to go upon the decks." But it was altogether a most
jovial occasion. The hospitable daimyo proposed a
toast to the King of England, and insisted that the great
pint-and-a-half goblets of " Counterye wine " should be
drained to the last drop, sending one of his men about
the ship to make sure that everyone followed his orders.

On his next visit this irrepressible host brought with
him several women of his household, gowned in rich,
silk kimonas and with their faces powdered and painted,
their teeth completely blackened. At first they were
bashful and retiring in the presence of the English
sailors, but the daimyo " willed them to be frolicke,"
so they sang and played upon " certain instruments
whereof one did much resemble our lute."

One curious incident occurred at this time which
rather pathetically illustrates the status of the Catholic
converts in Japan. " I gave leave to divers women of
the better sort," Captain Saris writes in his journal, " to
come into my Cabbin, where the picture of Venus,
with her sonne Cupid, did hang somewhat wantonly
set out in a large frame. They, thinking it to bee Our
Ladie and her sonne, fell downe and worshipped it,
with shewes of great devotion, telling me in a whispering
manner (that some of their own companions, which were
not so, might not heare), that they were Christianos :
whereby we perceived them to be Christians, converted
by the Portugal Iesuits."

Almost every day there was an exchange of visits
between the Japanese and the wondering Englishmen.
The former would board the " Clove " and leaving their
shoes on deck make their way to the cabin, where
the ship's officers would be gathered. Then clapping
their hands, " and so wagging or moving of their heads
a little to and fro, they stooping, steppe with small

steps sideling from the partie saluted and crie 'Augh, Augh.'" The company would then squat down on satin and velvet mats and there would be great wining and dining on wild boar and *sake*. One time the Englishmen were entertained with a theatrical performance. The daimyo brought with him to the " Clove " a company of women who " were actors of comedies, which passe there from island to island to play, as our players doe here from towne to towne, having severall shifts of apparrell for the better grace of the matter acted."

It was not uncommon for theatrical performances to be given aboard the ships of the East India Company, though this was most certainly the first time one had ever been presented by a company of Japanese players. It was usually the sailors themselves who acted, and we can read in the journal of a certain Captain Keeling, that he permitted this diversion " to keepe my people from idlenes and unlawfull games, or sleepe." The comedies or tragedies most often played were those of a new playright who was making a great success in London. On September 5, 1607, Captain Keeling allowed his men aboard the " Dragon," Lancaster's old ship, to put on one of these new plays. It was " Hamlet." [20]

Finally Adams arrived at Hirado. A queer situation then developed. For thirteen years the exile had been longing to see some of his fellow countrymen and here at last they were. But he found that somehow the reality did not live up to his dreams. He found that the ties which should have bound him to these Englishmen were extremely slight, and that their ways were so different from his ways that they had little in common. Although he had not realized it, his long isolation in Japan had made his fellow countrymen greater strangers than the Japanese.

Furthermore, there was immediate friction between
Adams and Captain Saris. The latter was an arrogant and
overbearing man. He tactlessly patronized the English
exile and showed that he was going to override whatever
advice Adams might give him, despite his instructions.
He seemed to think that he knew more about Japan
than the man who had lived there so long, and he was
openly suspicious of the Pilot's friendship with the
Japanese as he showed in writing in his journal that
Adams gave " so admirable and affectionated commendatyons of the Counterye as it is generally thought
emongst us that he is a naturalised Japanner."

Captain Saris was unjust in believing that Adams'
friendship for the Japanese and coolness towards the
Englishmen meant that he had foresworn his loyalty
to his native land. He still loved England, though
unfortunately he could not love these Englishmen. But
there developed a gulf between Adams and the new-
comers, quickly drowning the enthusiasm with which
the Pilot had hurried from Iyeyasu's Court to meet them.
When they presented him with some gifts from England
—a white hat and band, a Holland shirt, stockings and
silk garters, and a pair of slippers—he could not be
enthusiastic over these symbols of a life which now
seemed further away than ever. When "many pro-
fering after he came downe to go along with him in
love, he intreated the contrarye." But it was not so
much, as they thought, that he felt them " not good
enoffe to walke with him," but that he was unable to
reconcile himself to these new circumstances so quickly.

He was proud and inclined to hold himself aloof,
perhaps, but deeper than that was the change which
had come over him during the long years in Japan. It
is pathetic to read that when the English asked him to
dine with them and to tell their cook " what dyatt he
best affected," he declined and went off by himself

to the Japanese house where he had hung his colours,
" a Saint George made of coarse cloth."

But his personal feelings did not for a moment affect
his desire to help the new-comers and to do whatever he
could to establish the trade which was the object of their
voyage. He immediately told Captain Saris he would
intercede for them with Iyeyasu and urge him to grant
them extensive privileges. In fact, he prepared to set
out at once for the Shogun's Court.

Since Captain Saris was an envoy of King James the
journey was made with some pomp and ceremony.
There were nineteen in the party, ten of them Englishmen. Captain Saris and Adams were carried in palanquins, the seamen rode on horseback, and the Japanese
attendants followed on foot, some of them leading
horses laden with the presents which had been brought
for Iyeyasu and samples of the goods the Englishmen
hoped to sell to his people. According to the custom
of the country a Japanese bearing a pike marched at
the head of the little procession.

Their way led them along the Tokkaido, the great
road which the Shogun had had built between Kyoto
and Yedo and one of the two which the daimyos coming
to Court were required to follow. It was lined with
tall, sombre firs and was always carefully swept. Cedar-
wood bridges spanned the many mountain streams.

Everywhere along the Englishmen's route were
crowds of travellers. They met daimyos and samurai
also proceeding to the capital with their long trains
of followers : pikemen, footmen, guards and servants
all marching in order. The chief officers in large straw
hats, cloaks and wide breeches, sat cross-legged upon
led horses ; the daimyo was borne in a palanquin carried
by eight men, his umbrella-bearer and his hat-bearer
walking beside him. There were sometimes as many
as a thousand retainers in the retinues of these feudal

chieftains, and as they passed by the common people
kneeled in the road. Also there were on the Tokkaido
beggars by the score and pilgrims by the hundred, begging nuns with painted faces and shaved heads.

Fifty-seven stations where horses were kept for the
post and lodgings and provisions provided for the
travellers were located along the road. Jugglers,
musicians, singers and hawkers thronged the little
villages of thatch-roofed wooden houses opening wide
upon the street. Temples stood in quiet groves of
firs with the torii at their entrances glittering with little
strings of white paper, votive offerings to the Shinto
gods or to the Buddha. Everywhere were pedlars
offering their wares of straw shoes, sweetmeats, tooth-
picks and fans marked with road directions and the
distance to the next inn, with its prices, fixed by law,
for food and lodging. Painted wenches sat at the
doors of the refreshment houses and subtly beckoned to
the passers-by.

Under the lead of Adams the cavalcade of Englishmen pressed on as fast as it could, with the marvelling
seamen amazed at the signs of prosperity and order
they saw on every hand. They spent their nights in
the larger towns, where watchmen sounded each hour
with a different musical instrument and their Japanese
hosts, who knew Adams well, feasted them with rice,
fish, beans, wild fowl, deer, boar and pigs. They
drank the Japanese wine, and Captain Saris had difficult
work keeping track of his men. They enjoyed only
too well the hospitality of the country and their fiery
cups of *sake*.

Beyond Osaka the party turned off the Tokkaido and
went down toward Surunga—another town which we
are told was as large as London—where Iyeyasu had
retired while his son held Court at Yedo itself. In
passing they saw the great Daibutsu, the famous statue

YEDO

From Montanus' "Ambassades Memorables"

of the Buddha which still stands at Kamakura, and some
of the Englishmen " went into the bodie of it, and hoope
and hallowed, which made exceeding great noyse."
As forerunners of the countless tourists who have
followed their lead they carved their initials on its
bronze sides.

At Surunga, Adams took it upon himself to secure
their reception by Iyeyasu. The Shogun was glad to
welcome traders from England, and after the delicate
question of whether Captain Saris should give his
letter from King James directly to Iyeyasu or to his
Court secretary had been decided in favour of Japanese
custom, the Englishmen had their audience. Captain
Saris presented his gifts—an uninspiring selection of
clothes and two cups, one of silver and one of gilt,
a present hardly calculated to interest Iyeyasu as much
as had the two brass fire engines brought by the Dutch
some years before—and then withdrew leaving the
actual negotiations in Adams' hands.

The Pilot urged his country's cause with enthusiasm
and persuaded the Shogun to meet England's request
for full trading privileges throughout his empire. So
successful was he that the charter Iyeyasu granted the
new-comers gave the English more rights and greater
liberty than any other foreigners enjoyed. The Shogun
also entrusted to Adams an answer to the letter from
King James, which ended with the homely advice to
the English king, " take care of yourself at this change
of season."

The purpose of his visit achieved, Captain Saris went
on to pay his respects to Iyeyasu's son at Yedo and then
returned to Hirado by way of Kyoto. He had hoped
to have audience with the " pope," who held his ceremonious but empty Court at Kyoto ; but this was
impossible. Adams never saw the real emperor ; even
the ministers of the Shogun when they came to pay

their respects to the descendant of the gods saw only
a dark figure behind a semi-transparent curtain. This
nebulous figure and his twelve consorts lived a secluded
and futile life stifled in the effeminate atmosphere of
poetry contests, tea ceremonies and flower arrangement.

At Hirado Captain Saris hurried ahead with his preparations to return to England, having arranged to
leave a number of English merchants, headed by Richard
Cocks, to establish the factory which would serve the
East India Company as a base for its new commerce.
The chance to exchange England's chief products of
cloth and lead for Japan's gold and silver was a godsend
to the Company. The great drawback to trade with
the Indies had been its drain upon England's slender
supply of gold. Here was the best opportunity in the
East to redress this unfavourable balance by developing
a market which really seemed suited for English goods.

The question now arose as to what Adams should
do. At last he had a chance to return to England, for
not only did Captain Saris have instructions to offer
him passage home on the "Clove," but in his last interview with Iyeyasu the Shogun had finally granted him
permission to leave Japan. But the opportunity had
come too late. Adams now decided that he would
stay in his adopted country.

There are perhaps three explanations of his decision.
Adams advanced as one of them his comparative poverty.
He had little to show for his long years of exile except
his farms at Hemi-Mura, and he may have thought that
by remaining in Japan, now that trade with England
had been inaugurated, he could soon win a measure
of profit that would enable him to return somewhat
later to better advantage. Furthermore, his fondness
for Captain Saris had not increased during the past
months, and he did not relish being beholden to him
for the passage home. The arrogant seaman had

refused to follow Adams' advice as to where the English
factory should be located, and had offended both him
and Iyeyasu by choosing Hirado instead of a site nearer
the Court. And there were other points of disagree-
ment, for Adams wrote the East India Company of
" discourtisses offred me by the generall, the relacion
whereof I leave to others."

But, more important than either of these considerations, the arrival of the English had shown him how
tenuous were his ties with home. He simply preferred
to remain in Japan. He never admitted this ; but on
the other hand he never again talked of returning,
although throughout the rest of his life English ships
called regularly at Japanese ports, and scarcely a year
went by without an opportunity for him to take passage
to England. He had really become a " naturalised
Japanner."

He did, however, agree to take service with the
East India Company, although even in this matter there
were differences with Captain Saris. Puerile haggling
over Adams' salary of a hundred pounds a year and
other disputes which the Pilot characterised as " thinges
to me veru strang and unlooked for," marked the
departure of the " Clove." And as his parting shot
Captain Saris instructed Cocks that the man who had
just obtained for the East India Company its favoured
position in Japan was " onlye fittinge to be mr. of the
junke, and to be used as linquist at corte." Happily
we can bring the account of this unfortunate phase of
Adams' relations with the English to an end by reporting
that Cocks in his first letter to the East India Company
wrote that he had found Adams " tractable and willing
to doe your Wor. the best service he may."

From Adams' own letters we now learn of the chief
motive which was responsible for his joining the Company, a motive which carries us back half a century, to

the days of Chancellor and Jenkinson. He hoped to
discover the North-east Passage. He hoped the East
India Company would equip an expedition which could
sail northward from Japan and make its way through the
Arctic seas to European waters.

There is a possibility that Adams may once have
sought the North-east Passage by the route followed
by Chancellor. He may have been with the expedition
sent out by the Prince of Orange under Cornelis Kyp,
which succeeded in reaching Spitzbergen in 1593. But,
whether or not he had already tried his hand at discovering a shorter route to the East than the long voyage
about Cape Horn or the Cape of Good Hope, it was an
ambition which fired his imagination as it had that of so
many Elizabethans. His zest for adventure had not
been killed by his years of comparative inaction in Japan.
The restless spirit which had led him to give up building
ships to sail them, to give up his trade off the Barbary
coast for the more hazardous voyage to the Indies,
simply flamed up anew as he thought of what he might
now be able to do. He was convinced that he could
find that will-o'-the-wisp which Englishmen had been
pursuing for over a century.

Adams had long conversations with the Shogun
about the possibility of the entrance to the North-east
Passage lying somewhere north of Japan. Iyeyasu
became as interested as Elizabeth herself would have
been and even went so far as to give the Englishman a
letter to the people of Yezo, the northernmost of the
islands of Japan, who Adams describes as " tartares,
joyning to the Cam, or border of Cattay."

Armed with this support the Pilot wrote enthusiastically, pleadingly, to the East India Company. He
begged them to send him the supplies to fit out an
expedition : cordage, canvas, tar, a compass, hour-
glasses, a pair of globes, " soum cardes or mapes

contayning the wholl world," and fifteen or twenty seamen
—" or less, it is no matter." " Thees things yf your
wourship do furnish me with," he wrote Sir Thomas
Smythe, " you shall find me not neglegent in such
honorabell surves : by God's grace." He was now
sixty years old, but all he wanted was half a dozen
British seamen, a compass and a map and he was ready
to set out again on uncharted seas in pursuit of a dream.

But, like Jenkinson, Adams was doomed to disappointment. England had had too many tragic experiences in its search for the North-east Passage, and
the East India Company was not willing to venture
another expedition. Adams received neither his seamen
nor his maps. Instead of sailing northward he had to
content himself with voyages to Siam and Cochin China
in the new trade which the Company was attempting to
open between these countries and Japan.

They were hazardous enough, as may be seen from
the entries of Adams' log-book. His first expedition,
in a junk appropriately named the " Sea Adventure,"
ended when he was blown off his course and forced to
seek haven in the Ryukyu Islands, which stretch down
from Japan toward Formosa. There he spent several
months in enforced idleness while the damage done his ·
ship was being patched up. There was some relief to
the monotony of this long wait in the constant quarrels
between his crew and the Japanese passengers on the
junk. At one time there was almost open battle—the
supercargo of the " Sea Adventure " led twenty of his
compatriots to the attack with pikes and swords—but
somehow Adams managed to restore order. By the
time the junk was again seaworthy it was too late in the
season to go on to Siam and they turned back to Japan.
The sole result of the voyage was that, in taking back to
Hirado some sweet potatoes, Adams introduced this
vegetable to Japan for the first time.

His next voyage was more successful. Again the "Sea Adventure" headed for Siam, sailed south along the China coast, rounded the cape of Indo-China, passed through the Gulf of Siam and made its way up the Menam River. Off what is now Bangkok it finally dropped anchor, and while the merchants prepared to barter their cargo of Japanese armour and weapons, fans and tunny fish, for Siamese deerskins and teakwood, Adams visited the Court of Siam's king at Ayuthia. He was cordially received and the gifts he bore from the East India Company were accepted, but he remained there only a few days. The "Sea Adventure" soon weighed anchor and made an uneventful return to Hirado.

When Adams reached Japan after this voyage he found that Iyeyasu was dead. The great Shogun had died in 1616 and his son, Hitetada, had taken his place.

For the Englishman this meant the loss of both a patron and a friend, and it was with a heavy heart that he hurried to Yedo to pay his respects to the new ruler and seek his confirmation of the trading privileges enjoyed by the English under Iyeyasu. But the Court no longer welcomed him with the old-time cordiality. He could not now brush past the daimyos and talk with their feudal overlord while they waited in his ante-chambers. He had to wait his own turn.

This does not mean that Adams was unpopular, for Hitetada was often to send for him, but he had lost his specially privileged position. On this first visit there was nothing for him to do but wait until the Shogun would see him, and for several days he did not dare to leave the Court for fear of missing Hitetada's summons.

Finally he was received and did his best to persuade the new Shogun to renew the English privileges. He thought he had succeeded, but a little while after he had left the Court an order was issued which showed that the

policy of Hitetada was not to be that of his father.   All
foreigners in Japan were now to reap the reward of the
disturbing activities of the Jesuits and to feel the effect
of that fear of foreign conquest which Adams himself
had helped to instil in the Shogun's Court.   Hitetada
decreed that the English trade should be closely restricted
to Hirado and Nagasaki.

This was a hard blow for the little factory.   It had
not proved too successful under the best conditions.
Captain Saris' failure to follow Adams' advice as to its
location, the poor judgment of those in England as to
the goods to be sent out for sale—an item in one
shipment was three dozen pairs of spectacles—and the
rivalry of the Dutch, who first undersold the English
and then captured their vessels, were among the factors
combining to dash the high hopes of the East India
Company for its Japanese trade.

With the activities of the factory so restricted and his
special influence at Court gone, Adams now decided to
leave the Company's employ.   He had traded a good
deal on his own account and his affairs had prospered.
While he always remained ready to help out the English
in any way he could, his official connection with them
was now severed.

His contacts with the English factory had never been
entirely happy.   The little community at Hirado lived
a life which could not have greatly appealed to him.
Its members were constantly worrying over the disposal
of their goods, rushing about to their Japanese agents
and haggling over prices, competing in bitter rivalry
with the Dutch.   They squabbled among themselves,
and with querulous complaints blamed Adams for
favouring other foreigners at their expense, or accused
him of failing to stand by them in their efforts to
win the favour of the Japanese.

Occasionally Adams would snap back at them in his

annoyance, then relent and invite them all to a dinner
and entertainment at his house.   He would provide an
elaborate Japanese feast and bring in dancing girls and
players.   Quantities of *sake* would be consumed, and
under the influence of this good-fellowship all their
differences would be forgotten.   Richard Cocks, who
perhaps the day before had complained bitterly of some
" unsezonable and unreasonable " letter he had received
from the Pilot, would write home enthusiastically that
he was now sure that he " could lyve with hym 7 years
before any extraordenary speeches should happen betwixt
us."

But Adams turned more and more to his Japanese
interests and his Japanese friends during these last years.
He still kept up his active life, going on several voyages
in his own interests, but when he returned to Japan
he would spend most of his time at Hemi-Mura, where
his children were now growing up.   Here he was known
and respected by his neighbours, here he was a samurai
whose word was law among his retainers and among the
peasants who worked his farms.   He was content with
the life he had created for himself in this country of which
he had scarcely heard when he had left England so many
years before.

So his days ran out their allotted course until at length
Richard Cocks wrote home in 1621, more than two
decades after the " Charity " had sailed from the Texel,
that " our good frend Capt. Wm. Adams, who was soe
longe before us in Japon, departed out of this world the
XVI of May last."

" In this lyf manny trobelles and afflixions," Adams
had once written, " and in the end death.   Thearfor it is
a blessed thing to dy in the Lord, with a faithfull trust
in God : for theay rest from theer labores."   In his will
there was one provision symbolical of the two loyalties
which had governed his life.   He bequeathed half of his

little estate to the family he had left in England in 1598 and never since seen, and half to his wife and children in Japan.

It was well that he died in 1620. The rulers of Japan were becoming more and more convinced that their country was in dire peril from the intrigues and plots of the Catholic missionaries and their converts. Hitetada saw no way of protecting Japan except by stamping out the new religion and barring all foreigners from the country. Three years after Adams' death the English voluntarily withdrew from their ill-fated factory, the Portuguese were closely restricted, and the Dutch confined to Nagasaki.

This was the beginning of the end. A few years more and by 1641 Japan was virtually isolated from the Western world. A handful of Dutch were allowed to retain a precarious foothold in their prison-like factory on the tiny island of Deshima, but otherwise not a single one of those foreigners who had been so hospitably welcomed for almost a century was allowed to land in Japan. No Japanese could leave the country on pain of death should he ever try to return. Christianity was fought with fire and sword. Japan had retired within herself, and this period of friendly intercourse with the nations of Europe came to an abrupt and tragic close.

V

SIR THOMAS ROE, 1581–1644

" Beinge a gentleman of civell behavior, of good bredinge, personage, and very good parts."

Minutes of the East India Company, 1614.

CHAPTER XIV

A ROYAL AMBASSADOR

WHILE the English trade which Adams had helped to introduce into Japan was doomed to failure, far-reaching success was to attend the ventures of the East India Company in another part of the world beyond the Cape of Good Hope. It was not long after Lancaster's first voyage that English ships anchored off the mainland of India and English merchants made their way to the glamorous Court of the Great Mogul. And when in 1615 King James sent out Sir Thomas Roe as the first royal ambassador " to any of those so farre remote eastern princes," there was forged the first link in a chain which was to bind Great Britain and India ever closer.

India had been known to England for many years. Not only had reports of its incredible wealth drifted to London through Portuguese channels, but long before the East India Company instructed one of Lancaster's successors to seek trade along the Malabar coast, English merchants had made their way overland to the Court of Akbar. The letters of these early travellers had, in fact, been one of the incentives for the organization of the Company and the despatch of its first expedition.

The first Englishman known to have visited India was Thomas Stevens. He had taken service with the Portuguese as a Jesuit priest and in time became rector of the Jesuit College at Goa, the capital of Portugal's Eastern empire. His letters to his father in London

first aroused interest in the possible trade England might
find in the Great Mogul's dominions and were largely
responsible for the departure for India, in 1583, of four
daring merchants.   These men, Ralph Fitch, John
Newbery, William Leedes, and James Story, made their
way overland to Goa.   Here they were thrown into
prison by the jealous Portuguese and only freed after
Stevens had intervened in their behalf.

Story stayed in Goa as a shopkeeper ; Newbery died
soon after setting out on the long journey back to
England ; Leedes pushed on to Agra and entered
the service of Akbar.   Only Ralph Fitch returned to
England to tell the miraculous story of travels which
had taken him to Akbar's Court, to Bengal, Siam and
many other parts of the Indies.   Then for the first time
from direct and unimpeachable sources England learned
of the splendour and magnificence of the Mogul empire.
The dreams of a legendary Cathay faded before the
actualities of an India which an Englishman had really
seen.   Here at last was the land where

> " the gorgeous East with richest hand
> Showers on her kings barbaric pearl and gold."

The next visitor to India was John Mildenhall, who
also travelled overland and was entrusted with a letter to
the Great Mogul from Queen Elizabeth.   Despite the
opposition of the Jesuits at Akbar's Court, who lost no
opportunity to proclaim that the English were " all
theeves," he succeeded in obtaining some sort of trading
privileges and returned confidently to London.

In the meantime, however, the East India Company
had determined to open up commerce with India, and it
was in 1608 that the first authorized attempt along these
lines was made by William Hawkins. [21]   Landing at
Surat, an important port on the western coast to the

north of the site of modern Bombay, this emissary of trade proceeded to Agra with a letter and a present from James I for the Emperor Jahangir, who had now succeeded Akbar on the Mogul throne.

Hawkins was at first cordially received. After he had shown his good faith by taking in marriage a " fayre mayden " out of Jahangir's harem, he was accorded the trading privileges which he sought for his nation. But his success was short-lived. Jealousy of his popularity turned the Portuguese into " madde dogges," and their intrigues, his own indiscretions, and Jahangir's scorn when he began to realize that Hawkins was only a trader, soon forced the Englishman to flee the Court.

It was only too apparent that the Emperor had no real interest in opening relations with England. As we shall later see, the contempt in which the Great Mogul held all those who engaged in commerce and his failure to appreciate the significance of trade with the West were for long insurmountable obstacles to the East India Company's plans. Jahangir had none of that far-sighted vision which characterized both Czar Ivan and Iyeyasu.

While Hawkins was falling into disgrace at Agra another English fleet had arrived off Surat under the command of Sir Henry Middleton. (22) On board one of these vessels the discredited Hawkins took refuge and aroused the indignation of the new-comers by his stories of the treatment he had received at the Mogul Court. A retaliatory attack was consequently made upon some Indian ships in the Red Sea, with the result that when a third English fleet came out, in 1612, under Thomas Best, it was received with respect and at least a show of cordiality.

If the hostility of the Mogul somewhat abated during this period, that of the Portuguese was revived. The ruler whom the Pope had appointed " lord of the naviga-tion, conquest and trade of Ethiopia, Arabia, Persia

and India " was aroused at England's encroachment
upon his preserves. Peace between England and
Portugal might be possible in Europe, but beyond the
Cape of Good Hope treaties had no effect. Portugal's
claim to domination of the entire East and England's
refusal to recognize her sovereignty except in cases of
actual possession could be reconciled only by force.
Two naval battles had to be fought off Surat between
English and Portuguese fleets before England was free
to renew her negotiations at Jahangir's Court.

In the first of these engagements Thomas Best won a
fierce fight against superior odds because of the excellence
of the British markmanship. " We danced the hay about
them so that they durst not show a man upon the
hatches," wrote this doughty sea-captain. The Portuguese ships were scattered or sunk, and their casualties
were variously estimated from 160 to 500 men in comparison with the loss of three English sailors.

It was a doubly significant victory because it won new
prestige for the English in India. The Mogul troops at
Surat were able to watch the fiercest of the engagements
in which the British were victors, " all the camp standing
by the sea-side looking on us." Best thus felt safe in
leaving a small colony of English merchants at Surat
with the hope that by renewing English representations
at Agra they might secure the trading privileges which
Hawkins had won and then so quickly lost.

But the struggle with Portugal was not over. When
Nicholas Downton followed Best's course to Surat in
1615, his fleet of four vessels and 400 seamen was
attacked by a Portuguese armada captained by the
Portuguese viceroy himself. Six great galleons, three
smaller ships, two galleys, and sixty rowed barges—the
whole fleet manned by 2,600 Portuguese and 6,000
natives—were massed against the tiny English force.
Yet such was the respect in which the Portuguese held

the British gunners that after three months of futile
manœuvring this powerful armada withdrew, without
having dared to launch any direct attack upon Downton's
four ships.

While English seamen had been establishing their
country's supremacy in the Indian Ocean, English
merchants had been miserably failing to win the Indian
trade. A succession of unofficial envoys had made their
way to Jahangir's Court, but no sooner did the Emperor
and his officials discover that they were traders than they
refused to have anything to do with them. It was a
situation far different from any that the English had
encountered in their other ventures. Chancellor and
Jenkinson had been merchants, as well as envoys of
Elizabeth, but were received all the more cordially by
Ivan on this account. Lancaster had traded with the
King of Achin. Adams had not lost favour with
Iyeyasu because of his interest in commerce. But at the
Court of Jahangir the haughty Mogul officials would
not demean themselves by any intercourse with men of
trade. " There pride is such," wrote one of the English
envoys despondently, " that they scorne them, making
no more reaconing of them then of the banyans, whome
they hold little better then slaves."

Nor did the attitude which these merchant-envoys
adopted help their cause. For the sake of their precious
trade they submitted to every insult, and became meanly
abject and fawning in the face of Mogul pride. No one
of them showed any of that independence so typical of
the English pioneers in Russia, Central Asia, the Spice
Islands and Japan.

There was for example William Edwards, the last of
this string of impotent envoys. When Sir Thomas Roe
finally arrived in India he reported that this merchant
" had suffered blowes of the porters, base peons, and
beene thrust out by them with much scorne by head

and shoulders, without seeking satisfaction ; and . . .
carried himselfe with such complacency that hath bredd
a low reputation of our nation."

Back in London the merchants were quick to realize
the seriousness of this situation. Something had to be
done if the English were to have any standing at all in
India. , And something had to be done at once, for the
scornful Emperor was showing more and more how
little he cared for English trade. He had given the
government of Surat to his son, Prince Khurram,
who was later to become Emperor Shah Jehan, and
no one at Court was more notoriously hostile to
the English. His party favoured the Portuguese in so
far as they favoured any foreigners, and his deputy
governor at Surat, one Zulfaker Khan, was known to be
intriguing to expel the English entirely from the Mogul
dominions. If the trade from which the London merchants hoped so much was to be established, Jahangir
had to be conciliated. Otherwise England might as well
withdraw from India altogether.

There was but one move which seemed to hold out
any possibility of friendly relations. Every letter from
India insisted upon it. And that step was simply the
despatch of an envoy to Jahangir's Court who would
be " a man sent immediately from our King." No
merchant could hope to win the Emperor's consent to a
trade agreement. A royal ambassador was England's
one chance.

Sir Thomas Smythe first broached the matter at a
meeting of the " committees " of the East India Company
on September 7, 1614. Plans had been made to despatch
a new fleet to India which was to be the finest and best-
equipped ever sent out, and it was proposed that it
should carry England's first ambassador to the Orient.
" Because there is and wilbe occasion of employinge
one of extraordinarye parts to reside att Agra to prevent

any plotts that may be wrought by the Jesuits to circum-
vent our trade," read the minutes of this meeting, " Mr.
Governor recommended to their serious considerations
the sufficiencye of Sir Thomas Rowe, a gentleman well
knowne unto them all to bee of pregnant understandinge,
well spoken, learned, industrious and of comelie personage, and one of whom there are greate hopes that hee
may worke much good for the Company."

Considerable debate was necessary before the decision
was ultimately made to adopt this suggestion. An
embassy seemed a tremendous expense to the canny
merchants. Also they were not sure of the attitude of
the King and feared royal interference in their affairs.
Yet the necessity of taking drastic measures to defend
their interests in India won them over, and they not only
approved their governor's plan but his selection of an
envoy. Sir Thomas Roe was appointed to the post and
a ready and willing sanction to the undertaking was
given by King James, who made the knight his official
ambassador. He was furnished with letters of credence
and a royal missive to the " Great Mogor, King of the
Orientall Indies, of Chandahar, of Chismer and Corazon,
etc."

Sir Thomas was peculiarly well-equipped to carry out
this important mission. Although he was a man from
an entirely different stratum of society than the merchants
and seamen who had opened English relations with
other parts of the East, he had much in common with
them. He had something of the Elizabethan spirit of
adventure and all of its independence, while his background and training gave him the added qualifications
of diplomatic skill and persuasive tact. As still another
asset for his ambassadorial rôle every contemporary
account lays emphasis upon his " comelie personage."
His portraits show that he would have been considered
distinguished-looking in any age.

Roe came from a noted city family ; his grandfather
had been Lord Mayor of London in 1568. From this
origin he inherited a shrewd knowledge of business and
a store of common sense, to which his early life added
unusual culture and experience of the world. He
studied at Magdalen College, Oxford, and spent some time
at one of the Inns of Court. Influential friends then
introduced him at Court, and he shortly was made an
Esquire to the Body by Queen Elizabeth. In the closing
years of her reign he continued to grow in favour and
within two years of the accession of James he was
knighted. Having as friends and patrons Prince Henry
and the Princess Elizabeth, later to become the Queen of
Bohemia, he had every reason to look forward to a
brilliant career at Court.

But, in 1610, when he was thirty years old, Roe
became fired with the restless enthusiasm for adventure
which had sent the courtiers of Elizabeth to the four
corners of the earth, and he decided to set out himself
upon a voyage of discovery. With the financial aid of
the Earl of Southampton and Sir Walter Raleigh he
equipped two pinnaces and sailed for Guiana. He
explored the coast of South America from the Amazon
to the Orinoco and penetrated three hundred miles up
the former river into the jungles of Brazil.

When he returned to England from this voyage a
series of events quite changed the direction of his life.
Prince Henry, who had been his closest friend at Court,
died in 1612, and a few months later Princess Elizabeth
was married. Roe decided to leave Court and enter
public life. He succeeded in being returned to Parliament as a member for Tamworth, but unfortunately his
views were too liberal to commend him very highly
to King James. He was offered no post in the Government which would enable him to maintain his rank and
position, a consideration now doubly important as he

SIR THOMAS ROE

had secretly married the daughter of Sir Thomas Cave of Northamptonshire.

It was in these circumstances that he was offered the post of ambassador to Jahangir and he did not hesitate to seize an opportunity which would both enable him to recoup his fortune and to bring his abilities to the attention of the Government.

So soon as the embassy had been definitely decided upon he set about preparing himself. His retinue was to consist of fifteen followers. A chaplain and a surgeon were provided by the East India Company while he himself engaged his servants. His own salary was six hundred pounds a year and the allowance for his men one hundred pounds, with thirty pounds for their livery.

Realizing how important the impression he might make at Jahangir's Court would be to the fulfilment of his mission, Sir Thomas carefully selected his servants' liveries and his own clothes. He spent lavishly, even drawing from his own pocket to supplement the Company's allowance. To his own wardrobe, for example, he added a suit of scarlet cloak and hose with a crimson satin doublet trimmed with gold lace ; others of sea-green velvet, of carnation and sea-green, of cloth of gold, and one of silver doublet and hose with a purple lined coat.

When on February 2, 1615, the company sailed in the " Lion," one of a fleet of four vessels under the command of William Keeling, Sir Thomas was prepared to show the Great Mogul that for all the magnificence of his Court there was a monarch in the West whose ambassador had every right to command his respect.

CHAPTER XV

THE GREAT MOGUL

THE voyage to India was virtually uneventful. The route was now well charted, and while the Portuguese might still resent English intrusions of their territory the dangers and hazards of the Indian Ocean had greatly decreased. The four ships of the East India Company fleet were able to stop at the Cape of Good Hope, at the Comoro Islands and at Sokotra for fresh provisions—" oxen and cowes . . . goats . . . Arabian sheepe . . . hennes . . . oranges, lemons, lymes in great abundance, which we bought for callicoes, hollands or other lynnen, sword blads, and rialls of eight." Rough weather was met off Sokotra when one of the vessels " shippt a sea into her mainetopp, and filld her betweene the decks, that shee was in great perill," but compared with Lancaster's first voyage about the Cape of Good Hope there was little to disturb the calm of the long and tedious days at sea.

Sir Thomas in fact was bored. He played on his viol. He wrote in his diary. [23] He amused himself by making his own calculations of the ship's position, exulting when they turned out to be more accurate than those of the navigators. But as he was not in command of the ship, as he had been on his voyage to South America, he grew restive with the enforced inaction. It was to his great relief that on September 18, seven months after they had left port, the four ships anchored in the roadstead off Surat.

Roe immediately found himself faced with a difficult situation, one which called forth all his tact and diplomacy. The opposition to English traders was still pronounced and his countrymen in such poor repute with the Mogul officials that their presence in India was barely tolerated. The factors in Surat whose business it was to obtain the fine Indian cloths, cotton and indigo which the East India Company sought in exchange for its shipments of English cloth, lead, tin, cutlery and glass, found their trade almost at a standstill.

Sir Thomas had no sooner landed than he decided that his only course was to take a firm and determined stand. He would insist upon the rights and privileges to which his countrymen were entitled and seek at Jahangir's Court a treaty which would on the one hand regularize their position and free them from the menace of Portuguese intrigue, and, on the other, afford them some surety against the petty annoyances and wanton interference to which they were subjected by the local Mogul officials. He would reassert the dignity of England, and by demanding the treatment due to a royal ambassador erase the impression created by that Company agent who had " carried himselfe with such complacency that hath bredd a low reputation of our nation." It was in short Roe's determination, as he wrote in the journal which he kept throughout his stay in India, " eyther to rectifye all or lay my life and fortune both in the ground."

It was not long before his policy was put to the test. Knowing nothing of the character of this new English envoy, the officials at Surat " laughd one upon another " at his pretensions to ambassadorial rank, and directed the customs agents to search both him and his followers before allowing them to enter the city. Roe indignantly refused to submit to such an affront. Somewhat taken aback by his vigorous and forceful demand to be treated as an ambassador of a King equal in power to their own,

the officials then suavely requested that they at least be
allowed to carry out the forms of this regulation for all
foreign visitors by " laying their hands " upon four or
five of the Englishmen " not as to search but to embrace
them."

In the interests of harmony Sir Thomas agreed to this,
only to realize that the officials were still intent on
exercising their authority and planned to express their
scorn of his embassy by enforcing their usual examina-
tions.   So he quickly rallied his men about him, called
for his pistols—" those were my frendes "—and prepared
to defend his rights, if necessary with his life.   The
astounded officials at last realized that this was a new
manner of Englishman.   They hastily abandoned their
attempt to search his men and begged him to forget the
incident, " that all was mistaken."

If this was the first lesson, others were still necessary
to convince Zulfakar Khan, the governor of Surat, that
the new envoy was an ambassador determined upon
treatment as an ambassador.   This haughty and
avaricious official insisted that Roe should pay him a
formal visit before proceeding to the Emperor's Court.
Sir Thomas flatly refused.   Finally the governor was
forced to give in on this point of ceremony and his
curiosity and interest led him to call upon the Englishman.

But the duel for prestige was not yet over.   When
Zulfakar Khan, resplendent in an elaborate Persian robe
of cloth of gold, was met by Sir Thomas at the door of
the Englishman's house, " he goeing rudely like a horse
forward, gott before me."   Whereupon the ambassador, not to be out-tricked, brusquely passed him and
upheld his higher rank by leading the Mogul official
across the courtyard.

The governor was compelled to recognize Roe's
status as a royal ambassador, but he continued to follow
a vacillating policy of wilful annoyance followed by

childish gestures of reconciliation. One day he would cause the ambassador's baggage to be broken into ; on the next he would send him " an oliphant to ride upon with footemen with flaggs and pendents." Sir Thomas refused to have any official relations with him, telling him bluntly that he was " no baby to be abused one day ; and pleased with a pageant the next," and finally left Surat determined to complain of this discourteous treatment when he reached the Emperor's Court. Jahangir had sent him a free conduct for the journey inland, and too late Zulfakar Khan tried to make amends for his insults, " desiring my friendship, and offered me anything I would demand."

The journey from Surat to Ajmere, where the Emperor was then holding Court, took over seven weeks. It was a miserable experience for the Englishmen. The merciless Indian sun, the dust and dirt of the country roads, the filthy surroundings of the little villages of closely-packed mud houses where they were forced to stop, the cramped, dirty, oven-like lodgings put at their disposal by the local officials, all combined to make their life almost unbearable. The great wealth of Ind was most certainly not reflected in the countryside. " The cuntrye is all slavish. . . . Your swyne lye better then any man," Sir Thomas wrote home. " And what I endure I best knowe."

One member of the party, an Englishman who had the high ambition of travelling on from India to Peking and carried a letter to the Emperor of China from King James, died on the way. Many others were ill. On one stage of the journey Sir Thomas himself was so prostrated by fever " as at night I was past sence and given over for dead ; but God raysed me."

The little cavalcade of Englishmen with their Indian servants travelled on horseback, their baggage in bullock carts. One of their greatest difficulties was a heavy

English coach which they were taking to Ajmere as a
present to the Emperor. At night they set up tents in
the fields whenever possible rather than camp in the
cities, and at every halt they were given the protection of
horsemen and foot-soldiers provided on the Emperor's
orders. Two weeks were spent at Burhanpur, where
Sir Thomas was received by Prince Parwiz, the Great
Mogul's second son, but otherwise few halts longer than
a day were made, for the entire company was anxious to
reach Ajmere and bring the comfortless journey to
an end.

On Christmas Eve, 1615, they finally entered the
capital, " coming in privately in the evening." Sir
Thomas was carried in a palanquin so ill that he could
not sit up.

As soon as he had somewhat recovered from the almost
disastrous effects of this trip he was summoned by the
Emperor. Jahangir's curiosity about the new envoy
who had so boldly flouted his officials at Surat could not
be long restrained, and the audience with the first English
ambassador was held at the daily durbar in the court of
the Mogul palace.

The Emperor, in " great but barborous state," sat
in a little gallery overlooking the crowd of courtiers
and common people gathered below him. His white
gown with its flowing skirt was bound about the waist
with a crimson sash and his feet and legs were wrapped
in rich leggings. Strings of pearls were wound about
his golden turban, his necklaces and bracelets glittered
with great diamonds and rubies, and his rings flashed
with gems of incredible size and brilliance. Two slaves
in calico stood beside him upon the heads of wooden
elephants driving away the flies with jewelled fans.

Beneath him on a slightly raised platform were the
officers of the Court and foreign ambassadors, almost as
richly gowned as the Emperor, while the body of the

A DURBAR

From "Voyages de Francois Bernier" contenant description des Etats du Grand Mogul

court was crowded with gentry and common people.
Sir Thomas described the brilliant scene as like a stage,
with its background velvet and silken canopies held
aloft by silver poles, on which the Emperor and his
courtiers strutted their brief hour before the crowd
packed into the pit to look on and admire.

The ambassador, accompanied by some of his staff,
entered the Court with what pomp and ceremony he
could.   We may imagine him in his suit of scarlet, his
doublet of crimson satin trimmed with gold lace, as he
made his way slowly along the lane which the courtiers
opened up to allow him to pass, his sword at his side
and his head held high.   At each of the rails in the
courtyard which separated the common people from the
gentry he made a respectful bow to the Emperor, and
another when two attendant slaves led him just beneath
the Great Mogul's gallery.   Then he handed the Emperor
the letter he bore from King James.

Jahangir read this document, which had been translated, with some curiosity, but he was more interested
in the next phase of the ceremony—the presentation of
the English gifts.   He graciously accepted the coach
with its lining of red velvet, a pair of virginals (the
seventeenth-century precursor of the piano), some
knives, a richly embroidered scarf, several gilded looking-
glasses and a sword.   Whereupon after solicitous inquiry
about the ambassador's health, offering to send him his
own physician, he dismissed Sir Thomas " with more
favour and outward grace . . . then ever was sheowed
to any ambassador, eyther of the Turke or Persian, or
other whatsoever."

He dismissed the ambassador, but he ordered the
English coachman and the English musician in Roe's
company to remain, and no sooner was the durbar over
than he came down into the courtyard to inspect his
new gifts with their help.   Getting into the coach he had

himself drawn about in it, and delighted in the ease and comfort with which he could ride. Then, although it was ten o'clock in the evening, he hurriedly sent for Sir Thomas that the ambassador might show him how to wear his new scarf and sword in the English manner, " in which he tooke so great pryde that he marched up and downe, draweing yt and flourishing."

This Eastern monarch who had so impatiently awaited the gifts brought from England, and then like a child with a new toy paraded up and down his Court playing soldier, was a great ruler. Ten years before Roe's arrival he had fallen heir to the empire of Akbar, and, although some of the unruly princes of the Deccan refused to acknowledge his power, all of northern Hindustan was under the iron hand of his control. His title of " World-Grasper " or " Conqueror of the World " was given some substance by the tributes paid him by neighbouring kings and princes. The envoys of Persia and Turkey prostrated themselves before him on their visits to his Court and presented him with velvets, tapestries and carpets, silken hangings and chests of jewels. His own subjects always paid him dutiful obeisance. The Rajah of Bijapur, who once dared to challenge his authority, made his submission with a gift of thirty-six elephants, whose chains were of copper, silver and beaten gold, fifty richly furnished horses, and pearls and rubies to the value of ten lakhs of rupees.

In the light of such obsequious respect the quiet bearing of the English ambassador and the meagreness of his gifts stood out in sharp contrast. But Sir Thomas had insisted that he would come to Court and pay his respects to Jahangir according to English custom. When he had been asked to prostrate himself before the Emperor he had proudly answered that he was " free from the custome of servants." He staked the prestige of his country on the independence and dignity of his own bearing, not on the value of his presents, and there is no doubt that Jahangir was at last forced to recognize in him the envoy of a monarch as proud as himself by the sheer weight of Roe's character. It was with a keen insight into the Mogul temperament that by disdaining to smooth his way by the " base creeping and bribing " practised by his predecessors, Sir Thomas won the respect which he otherwise might never have been paid.

As time went on he was received more and more into the Emperor's favour and his presence at the various Court ceremonies, all of which are duly described in his journal, gave him a unique opportunity to observe the life and character of this son of the line of Babar who sat on the Mogul throne.

Jahangir was a man of fantastic whims and strange contradictions of character. He was a cruel tyrant, a great hunter, a drunkard. And at the same time he was a just ruler, a lover of animals, and a poet of real feeling and artistic appreciation. One day he might cause a woman to be buried in the ground with only her head exposed to the piercing heat of the Indian sun, or throw some petty offender to his wild elephants and enjoy the spectacle of his horrible death. On another he would be humane and merciful and Sir Thomas would write that he found him " gentle, soft and good of disposition."

The Emperor once boasted in his diary, [24] that he had killed in the hunt 17,177 birds and animals, including 86 tigers, 64 wolves, 889 blue bulls and 36 wild buffaloes. Yet he erected a monument to a tame antelope and once even took the personal pains to devise a hot spray for his elephants when he found that they suffered from the winter cold. If he had drinking bouts every Friday night, he had religious discussions every Thursday.

He was fond of the verses of Omar Khayyám and referred in the diary to his own " poetical disposition."
Sir Thomas is the authority for the statement that he
was " of countenance cheerfull, and not proud in nature,
but by habitt and custome ; for at nights he is veary
affable, and full of gentle conversation."

Drinking was perhaps his greatest vice, an over-indul-
gence common to the whole line of Mogul rulers. As a
young man he was accustomed to take twenty cups a
day, and became so much a victim to this habit that he
wrote himself " that in the crapulous state from the
trembling of my hand I could not drink from my own
cup, but others had to give it to me to drink." He
later became more moderate, but throughout his life he
held weekly orgies which in a large measure accounted
for that perverseness in his character which made him,
when crossed, viciously cruel.

There was little statesmanship in the character of
Jahangir when questions of foreign relations arose.
If he was consistently friendly to Sir Thomas, asking him
to attend all the Court ceremonies and even his drinking
bouts, it was because he came to like the ambassador
personally. He had no real conception of the importance of the country Roe represented or of the significance to India of this new contact with Western civilization. Unlike Iyeyasu, who was interested in everything concerning the West, Jahangir was merely curious
about England's drinking customs or the rarities the
ambassador might bring him from Europe.

He was at one time especially delighted by two mastiffs
which were sent out by the East India Company. When
one of them attacked an elephant and fastening its teeth
in the elephant's trunk " made that huge beast extremely
to roare," the Emperor was beside himself with admiration for bulldog tenacity. He had four servants assigned
to care for each of the dogs—to carry them about in

palanquins and fan away the flies. Occasionally he would have them brought before him and feed them himself with silver tongs. A little later he got it into his head that above everything else he wanted an English horse " of the greatest size," and promised Sir Thomas that if one were brought him he would willingly grant all the English demands.

The daily life of the Emperor was made up of a succession of Court ceremonies. In the morning Jahangir showed himself to his people at the exact hour of sunrise ; at noon he watched the fights of elephants which " justle together like two little mountaines " ; in the afternoon he held official Court and heard whatever suits might be brought before him ; and in the evening " hee descends into a court ; on a throune hee discourseth and drincketh with much affabilitye." This schedule, Sir Thomas wrote, was as regular " as a clock that stricks at sett howers . . . the rest of his motion is inward amoung woemen, of which sort, though hee keepe a thowsand, yet one governs him, and wynds him up at her pleasure."

The lady to whom Roe refers was the famous Nur Mahal, whom Jahangir had married after a romantic love-affair. Her influence at Court was paramount, and the English ambassador had to take special pains to win her favour. So much was Jahangir her slave that coins were struck in her name, and Sir Thomas gives one instance of a time when intrigues divided the royal household and the Emperor had " fallen downe and taken his mistris by the feete to obteyne her leave to see his sonne."

One great occasion of the Mogul Court was Jahangir's annual birthday celebration. Sir Thomas was duly invited and has left us a vivid description of a scene which more than anything else impressed him with the incalculable riches and unrivalled magnificence of this

Eastern potentate.   Here was the basis for seventeenth-
century England's idea of the wealth of Ind, of the
barbaric splendour of the Mogul rulers.

All the high nobles of the realm gathered in an open
court of the palace, where they sat on velvet carpets
beneath spreading shade trees.   At one end of the
garden was a pair of scales made of heavy gold and set
with rubies and turquoises.   Upon this carefully prepared stage, brilliant with the gorgeous costumes and
jewels of the Court officials, entered with due ceremony
the Great Mogul.   He was clothed, wrote Sir Thomas,
" or rather loden, with diamonds, rubies, pearles, and
other precious vanities, so great, so glorious! . . . his
head, necke, breast, armes, above the elbows, at the
wrists, his fingers every one with at least two or three
rings, fettered with chaines, or dyalled diamonds,
rubies as great as wal-nuts (some greater) and pearles
such as mine eyes were amazed at."

Seating himself cross-legged on the golden scales
Jahangir was then weighed six times, against silver,
against gold and precious stones, against cloth of gold,
silk, linen, spices, and finally against grain, butter and
corn.   All of this wealth was later to be distributed
among his people.   He then mounted his throne and
taking basins of nuts, almonds and all kinds of fruit
fashioned out of thin silver, he threw them to his
courtiers.   " Great men scrambled prostrate upon their
bellies," but the dignified English ambassador would
not stoop so low.   Seeing this Jahangir filled his cloak
with a whole basin of silver.   Even then Sir Thomas
managed to keep only a small handful from the covetous
nobles who grabbed what they could.

In the afternoon of this important day the Emperor's
elephants, with chains and bells of gold and silver,
blankets of silk, and breastplates set with jewels, paraded
before him, and as each one passed beneath the throne

THE BIRTHDAY CEREMONY

From "Voyages de François Bernier"

it made " reverence very handsomly." Sir Thomas
stood beside the Great Mogul, still amazed at this wanton
display of wealth, and with eager eyes " saw what was
to be seene : presents, elephants, horses, and many
whores."

Drinking in the evening wound up the birthday
celebration. About ten Roe was summoned and found
Jahangir sitting on a little throne in a room of utterly
fantastic magnificence. It was so filled with rich furniture and trappings that the ambassador described it as
" rather patched then glorious, as if it seemed to strive
to shew all, like a ladie that with her plate sett on a
cupboard her imbrodered slippers."

Sir Thomas was immediately asked what he would
have to drink and diplomatically replied whatever he
was commanded, hoping it would not be " to much nor
too strong." In this he was disappointed. Jahangir
sent him a great flagon of wine, bidding him drink
twice, thrice, four or five times in his honour. Sir
Thomas did his best, but it was " more strong then ever
I tasted, so that it made me sneese." The Emperor
was in high spirits, and the spectacle of the dignified
English ambassador sneezing over his wine appealed
to him immensely in this jovial mood. He sent word
to Sir Thomas to keep his wine-cup, a vessel of pure
gold with a setting of jewels, as a remembrance of the
birthday, and he told Roe enthusiastically that he
esteemed him more " then ever any other Francke."

The riotous party ended only when the Emperor,
who " had been very busy with his cupps . . . suddenly
fell asleepe." The candles were then " popped out "
and Sir Thomas groped his way out of doors.

CHAPTER XVI

SPLENDOUR AND INTRIGUE

SIR THOMAS describes the varied scenes at Jahangir's Court vividly, but he did not wholly approve of them; nor did he find the other phases of his life at Ajmere too pleasant.

"All this greatnes, compared and weighed judiciously," he once wrote, "is like a play, that serves more for delight and to entertayne the vulgar then for any use." As a free and liberal Englishman he was incensed at the contrast between the wealth of the Court and the poverty of the people, who were not allowed to own land and were consequently virtual slaves of the Emperor's every whim. As a sincere Christian he was troubled by the paganism of the Hindus "in following sundry idolatryes and worshiping the creatures of heaven and earth promiscuously." Whatever may have been the reaction of Prince Charles to a letter in which Roe described the Mogul Court, the ambassador was reflecting his own feelings when he wrote: "Your Highnes cannot but bee weary to heare of soe much iniquitye; chast eares are defiled with the noyse of evill."

In his life apart from attendance at Court Sir Thomas was even less happy because his constant preoccupation with his diplomatic mission and with his task of restoring English prestige set him apart in lonely isolation. He made no friends with the Mogul courtiers, whose only interest in him lay in the possible gifts he might make them. He might entertain occasionally, and in turn was entertained with "very good respect, very good words, and very good meate," but such affairs were purely formal. Roe never learned to speak either Persian or Hindustani. Unlike William Adams, in Japan, he remained throughout his three year stay in India an absolute foreigner who touched only the surface of Indian life.

Together with his English companions he lived in a native mud house to which had been added "upon canes, a doozen thatched roomes." So far as possible they made their home like the houses to which they were accustomed in England. It was fitted out with English furniture—and their Indian guests never got over their amazement at seeing chairs and tables—while all their meals were prepared and served in English style. They had plentiful supplies—fish, game, fowl and all kinds of fruits, including the unfamiliar pineapple "which seemes to the taster to be a pleasing compound made of strawberries, claret wine, rose-water, and sugar, well tempered together." For drink they had the native wines and coffee—"a blacke seed boyled in water, which doth little alter the taste of the water . . . more healthful then pleasant."

Sir Thomas missed his English wines, for he could not abide the strong Indian spirits and complained that the water made him very ill. He missed his tobacco. [25] And the whole company were greatly troubled by the flies and "musquatoes" which were "ready to cover our meate as soone as it is placed on the table."

His retinue invariably wore their English clothes and despite the intense heat went abroad in doublet and hose. It was all a part of the ambassador's campaign to impress the Mogul Court; and when he himself went out it was always with a company of twenty-four footmen and guards.

Daily prayers were always held in the common dining-room of the English house. Sir Thomas insisted on everyone's attendance, and these services meant so much to him that when his chaplain, the Rev. John Hall, died, as did so many of the little English colony, he hurriedly wrote home to the East India Company that if a substitute were not sent out at once he would have to return, for " heere I cannot live the life of an atheist."

It was, all in all, a dull existence for Sir Thomas without companions whom he could meet on terms of social equality. He missed the life to which residence at the Courts of James and Elizabeth had accustomed him, and he missed the " conversation and the presence of those friends I love and honour." He had his quarrels with the English merchants carrying on the trade of the East India Company ; he suffered from recurrent attacks of the fever which had first assailed him on the over-land trip to Ajmere—in his first year he had " seven cold agues, two fevers " ; and he fell into such deep dejection that he wrote home dolefully that the Mogul capital was " the dullest, basest place that ever I saw and maketh me weary speaking of it."

He did have, however, at least one visitor who broke the monotony of life at Ajmere. This was the eccentric English traveller, Thomas Coryat, whose delicious book of European travel, " Coryate's Crudities, hastily gobbled up in five moneths' travells," had amused both the Court of James and the devotees of the Mermaid Tavern. Coryat had come to India on foot through Egypt, Turkey, Palestine and Persia. Once he had found his way to Jahangir's Court he soon distinguished himself.

On one occasion he made a long and flattering oration before the Emperor in Persian, and Jahangir rewarded him as he would have a Court fool by throwing him a

purse. This, it must be admitted, annoyed Roe, always
so solicitous of English dignity. Another time Coryat
had an altercation with the Hindu laundress of the
English colony, and so eloquently could he handle the
native Billingsgate that to the delight of his large audience
he effectively drowned the voice of his rival. Still
another outbreak of this erratic genius might have had
serious results. He climbed to the minaret of a mosque
and at evening prayer boldly called out in the tones
of a muezzin : " No God but one God, and Christ the
Sonne of God." It was only because the Indian Moslems
tolerantly judged that he was not wholly responsible
for his escapades that he escaped from this adventure
with his life.

Naturally this was not the type of man whom Roe
would have chosen for a companion in exile, but he
felt that here was someone whom the fates " have sent
hither to ease me," and let Coryat live in the English
house. The fantastic tales of the " greatest traveller
doubtlesse of the woorld " must have been some consola-
tion during the long Indian evenings. (26)

It was under these circumstances that Sir Thomas
endeavoured to carry out the mission on which the East
India Company had despatched him. He first tried
to secure redress for the injuries and insults which his
countrymen had suffered at Surat, and then urged upon
the Emperor a treaty granting the English free trade
throughout the Mogul dominions and " a good and
perfect, love, league and peace to endure for ever."
It was a difficult task. The Mogul Court was honey-
combed with corruption, and the ambassador found
himself blocked at every turn by Oriental duplicity—
" never had man to put up with soe much pride, covet-
ousnes and falsehood." Again and again his attempts
to bring his grievances to the attention of Jahangir
were side-tracked by the evasive promises of the scheming

12

courtiers through whom he had to carry on his official
business.

He faced definite and determined opposition in the anti-
English party of Prince Khurram, which was supported
by the influential Nur Mahal. They tried in every way
possible to prevent his placing his grievances directly
before the Emperor and spread false reports about
England's real intentions and the danger to the Empire
in admitting such perfidious foreigners. Sir Thomas
summoned his courage to " performe with an honest
hart all I had undertaken," but he felt he was futilely
throwing himself against a stone wall.

The most discouraging part of it all was that, if he
did succeed in obtaining the Emperor's ear despite the
wiles of his enemies, it did him little good. He floundered
in a sea of imperial indifference. Jahangir was friendly
enough, but he cared not a jot for treaties with England.
All he wanted was more presents from the East India
Company, English rarities which would impress his
subjects. He wanted more mastiffs, he wanted his big
horse, he wanted new toys.

Unfortunately Roe's presents were not enough to
satisfy him. He gave little enough in return, for Sir
Thomas once summed up the gifts he had received as
" hoggs flesh, deare, a theefe, and a whore," but Jahangir
was continually asking for his rarities. The ambassador
did the best he could. He advised the East India Company to send out table knives, swords, gilt armour,
precious stones, cloth of gold, looking-glasses, dogs,
wine, ostrich plumes, silk stuffs and " any rare knack
to please the eye," but for all his pains the Company
either sent out the wrong things or articles in such poor
condition that they were a disgrace. The merchants
in London did not realize how dependent were all their
hopes for a treaty on the Emperor's whims.

Some gilded looking-glasses once arrived, " unglued,

unfoyled, and fallen a peeices," others in leather cases were " rotten with mould on the outside and decayed within," while some telescopes were useless and a batch of pictures " not all woorth one penny." Sir Thomas was apologetic, but he could do nothing about it.

When a new consignment of goods would arrive from England the Emperor would often have it opened before Roe knew it had even come. He would then summon the ambassador and have it unpacked, asking pointedly for whom such and such an article was intended. Sir Thomas was invariably forced to make the diplomatic reply that it had been sent out for His Majesty if he would deign to take it. One time Jahangir found some hats for which Roe had sent for his personal use. The Emperor thought the women of his harem would like them. Away went the ambassador's hats. On another occasion Jahangir discovered a little whistle and contentedly blew away for an hour before he tired of it.

A treaty for trade? Jahangir would not demean himself by discussing such a thing. If Sir Thomas persisted he would find that the Emperor had fallen asleep. Once Roe threatened to leave India if he could get no satisfaction for the English demands, but Jahangir blandly told him: " If I would be gone, I might; if stay, I should bee welcome." It made no difference to the Emperor. He had no real concern with the English beyond his childish love for their gifts, and it is significant that the embassy is never once mentioned in his memoirs.

Sir Thomas grew more and more frantic. " This overgrowne eliphant," he wrote home in disgust, " will not descend to article or bynde him selfe reciprocally to any prince upon termes of equalety, but only by way of favour admitt our stay so long as it either likes him or those that governe him."

So matters dragged on. After Roe had been at Court

for a year the Emperor moved his capital to Mandu and then to Ahmadabad. His departure from Ajmere was very impressive.

Jahangir first took up his position at a palace window, and while two eunuchs fanned him with peacock feathers he distributed parting gifts, carefully lowered on silken strings to the admiring people gathered below. Roe had his usual place beside the Emperor, and for the first time since he had appeared at Court felt himself to be in the presence of the royal concubines. They were behind screens, but their curiosity about the English ambassador caused them to break little holes in them. Sir Thomas saw their fingers poking through, an eye glued to one of the apertures, or the shadowy figure of a woman glittering with strings of diamonds and pearls. When he looked up " they retyred, and were so merry that I supposed they laughd at mee."

Soon these same concubines came down into the courtyard and climbed to the gold-covered howdahs of their waiting elephants while the Emperor, his sword and buckler studded with diamonds, his plumed turban hung with a great uncut ruby, a diamond and an emerald, entered a coach which he had had copied from the one brought him by Roe. He was attended by the English coachman, in gaudy uniform, driving four horses. Two eunuchs rode on either side to drive off the flies. A company of soldiers with drums and trumpets preceded him, the Empress followed in another coach with twenty royal elephants, while the Mogul nobles, and among them Sir Thomas, walked with the royal procession as far as the palace gate.

Jahangir's first camp was but five miles outside the city, a wilderness of green and white tents surrounding the Emperor's brilliant red pavilion. A guard of elephants, almost a thousand strong, some of them with slings mounted on their backs which could hurl " a

THE GREAT MOGUL ON THE MARCH

From "*Voyages de Francois Bernier*"

bullet as bigg as a greaat tennis ball," guarded its approaches. Footmen with skins of water laid the dust along the royal path.

In the centre of all this splendour a throne of mother of pearl had been erected beneath canopies of cloth of gold. As soon as the Emperor arrived he mounted this throne, called for water to wash his hands, and then retired to his tent. The nobles went to theirs. "The vale," wrote Sir Thomas, "showed like a bewtifull citty . . . one of the greatest raretyes and magnificencyes I ever saw." Then he added rather sadly: "So I returned to my poore house."

When the Emperor travelled there were some 200,000 men, women and children in his company, and while on the march they covered eleven or twelve miles a day. If the ladies of his harem were not in the howdahs of the royal elephants they rode in "cradles hanging on the sides of dromedaries." Three thousand servants administered to Jahangir's wants, a thousand swordsmen formed his guard of honour. Every one of his royal elephants had seven grooms. A great troop of wrestlers was on hand to afford him amusement. Water from the Ganges was brought to him daily and ice supplied from the snow mountains by runners or post carriages.

Wherever he went, "throwgh woods and over mountaynes," Jahangir hunted. Sometimes he shot tigers from the back of an elephant and the Empress Nur Mahal once made the royal record of killing four tigers in six shots. At other times the hunt would be with leopards trained to drag down the game or with tame bucks which fought their own kind and by means of a rough noose attached to their horns, which became entangled in the antlers of the wild bucks, held their prey until the hunters arrived. So tame were these trained deer that they answered to a whistle.

Sir Thomas, of necessity, followed after Jahangir on

this expedition as soon as he could find carts and camels in the deserted city to carry his baggage. He caught up with the royal camp within a few days and pitched his tents, marked with an English flag, near those of the Emperor.

For eight months the Emperor stayed at Mandu, where the English established themselves in a deserted mosque. It was a desolate spot. Fires had to be burned at night to keep off the wild beasts and only by discovering a spring and keeping careful watch over their provisions did they save themselves from the hardships suffered by other camp followers. But, despite the want and actual starvation among his people when thousands of carts and camels had to be abandoned in the wooded hills, Jahangir kept up his royal state at all times. It was at Mandu that with great ceremony he received deputations from the princes of the Deccan who had been conquered by Prince Khurram, now rewarded for his valour with the title of Shah Jehan.

When the camp at length moved on to Ahmadabad conditions among the camp followers became even worse. The city was ravaged by plague. All of the English except Sir Thomas fell sick. Seven of the little party died.

For two years under such varying conditions of life the ambassador danced attendance on this roving monarch, growing at last " infinitely weary of this unprofitable imployment." It is true that by this time he had succeeded in obtaining from the Emperor some compensation for the losses his countrymen had suffered at Surat and they were at last free to carry on their trade without being subjected to the continual interference of the local Mogul officials, but he had hoped for more. Whatever privileges he obtained were gained only by firmans or general orders from the Emperor or from Shah Jehan.

Not once in all his months of Court attendance had
he been able to gain the Emperor's consent to a definite
treaty which would be of permanent value. He was
put off with one excuse after another until he at last
determined to make one final attempt and then return to
England with whatever concessions he could wring from
the reluctant Emperor.

Jahangir was about to strike camp and set off for Agra
when this interview took place. It resulted in his being
awarded a somewhat vague grant which provided for
" our reception and continuation in his domynons,"
and an additional firman from Shah Jehan which guaran-
teed the residence, freedom for trade and liberty to govern
themselves of the English merchants at Surat. It was
not as definite an agreement as Sir Thomas had hoped
to obtain, but it marked a tremendous advance over
any privileges the English had formerly enjoyed. The
ambassador was forced to be content. " Articles of
treaty on equall tearmes," he wrote home, " I cannot
effect ; want of presents disgraced mee."

Soon after this he took his leave of the Mogul Court
entrusted with a letter of friendship from Jahangir to
King James, which opened with the grandiloquent
phrase : " When your Majestie shall open this letter ;
lett your royall hart be as fresh as a sweete garden."

We have little record of Roe's return journey to Surat,
his four months' wait in the port for a ship to take him
home, or the long voyage back to England, but some
time in September, 1619, four and a half years after his
departure, he arrived in London. He was welcomed with
great ceremony by the governor and committees of the
East India Company who were more than satisfied with
the progress he had made in establishing relations with
India on a firm footing, and he was formally received
at Court by King James. On behalf of the Great
Mogul he presented his sovereign with " two antelopes,

a straunge and bewtifull kind of red deare, a rich tent, rare carpets, certain umbrellaes, and such like trinckets."

This brought Sir Thomas' mission to an end. Later he went as ambassador to the Ottoman Porte and was England's representative at the peace negotiations at Hamburg, Ratisbon and Vienna, services for his country which were rewarded by the Garter and membership in the Privy Council. Yet his opinions were still too liberal entirely to please Charles I, who had now succeeded James, and he was never offered that position in the Government to which both his achievements and his abilities entitled him. At the same time he was too loyal to the throne to cast in his lot with those who were planning to overthrow the King. He followed the only course which was open to him and retired from public life.

- " And at length," wrote a contemporary, [27] " this worthy person Sir Thomas Roe did after all his voyages and ramblings take a little breath ; but soon after, seeing how untowardly things went between the King and his Parliament, did willingly surrender it to Him that first gave it, on the 6th day of November in 1644, and two days after that his body was buried privately in the church at Woodford, near to Wansted in Essex."

With his later career we have no immediate concern, but what of the part he had played in India ? When he landed at Surat the English were in a precarious situation. They were threatened by the Portuguese, subjected to the wilful exactions of the local officials of the Mogul Court, and in danger of expulsion from India. English prestige was at its lowest ebb.

But, when he left, an entirely new relationship had been established between the English and the Mogul Court and as a matter of fact England had won a permanent foothold in India from which it was never to be dislodged. The Mogul officials were constrained by orders from the Emperor and his son to treat the English

with respect. Trading privileges had been confirmed
and if "articles of treaty on equall tearmes" had not
been effected, at least there was a definite understanding
between the English and the Mogul rulers. The letter
sent James by Jahangir was in itself striking evidence
that Sir Thomas had succeeded in re-establishing English
prestige in the Mogul dominions.

In all his dealings with Jahangir it is especially note-
worthy that Sir Thomas never suggested anything
remotely resembling force. The idea of conquest
which 150 years later was to govern England's relations
with India was completely foreign to this peaceful
ambassador. Throughout his stay in India he laboured
to convince Jahangir that all that England sought in
the East was trade. He did not favour force under
any circumstances—except against the Portuguese—
and often sent home to the East India Company the sage
advice that only by cultivating the friendship and respect
of the Mogul Court could the best interests of England
and English trade be promoted.

"A warr and trafique are incompatible," he wrote
to the merchants of London, pointing out that the
Portuguese were beggared by their military establish-
ments and never "profited by the Indyes, since hee
defended them," while the Dutch, "who seeke planta-
tions heere by the swoord," had fallen into the same
error. "Lett this bee received as a rule," Sir Thomas
declared, "that if yow will profitt, seeke it at sea, and in
quiett trade; for without controversy it is an error to
affect garrisons and land warrs in India."

In a letter written by Edward Terry, the chaplain
who had been sent out by the East India Company to
join Sir Thomas after the death of the Rev. John Hall,
we may find an apt summary of what Roe had accom-
plished in the unfavourable conditions which marked
his embassy.

"There can be," wrote Terry, "no dealing with this King upon very sure terms, who will say and unsay, promise and deny. Yet we Englishmen did not at all suffer by that inconstancy of his, but there found a free trade, a peaceable residence, and a very good esteem with that king and people; and much the better (as I conceive) by reason of the prudence of my Lord Ambassador, who was there (in some sense) like Joseph in the court of Pharaoh, for whose presence all his nation there seemed to fare the better."

NOTES

(1) The sixteenth-century chronicler of this voyage was Clement Adams, by whom, as Richard Eden tells us in " The History of Travayle " (London, 1577), the whole story was " largely and faithfully written in the Latine tongue." It is preserved in " The Principal Navigations, Voyages, Travels and Discoveries of the English Nation " (London, 1600) of Richard Hakluyt.

(2) In " Narratives of Voyages towards the North-West in Search of a Passage to Cathay and India " (Hakluyt Society, Vol. 5, London, 1849) by Thomas Rundall may be found interesting lists of the stores carried on these early voyages together with price lists of the merchandise exported.

(3) The enthusiasm of Thorne knew no bounds. He wrote a " booke " outlining his ideas which he sent to the British ambassador at Seville to supplement his petition to the King. It is a fascinating document. There was no need for him to append his apologetic comment : " I take license to be prolixious, and shalbe peradventure tedious."

(4) Evidence of English interest in Russia as early as the first year of the reign of Henry VII may be found in the record of a Court reception at which the Earl of Stafford and the Earl of Sussex appeared " in two long gounes of yelowe satin traversed with white satin and in every bend of whyte was a bend of cremson satin after the fashion of Russia or Russlande with furred hattes of greye on their heades, either of them having an hatchet in their handes and bootes with pykes turned up."

(5) The poet was William Warner, who in the period from 1586 to 1596 published a long narrative poem called " Albion's England." It is to be found in " The Works of the English Poets " (Vol. 4) published in 1801 by Alexander Chalmers.

(6) Jenkinson's travels may be found in Hakluyt and also in " Early Voyages and Travels to Russia and Persia by Anthony Jenkinson and other Englishmen " edited for the Hakluyt Society (Vols. 72 and 73) in 1886 by E. Delmar Morgan and C. H. Coote.

(7) The white cow of Cathay was the yak, which Marco Polo

refers to as an animal " very beautiful to sight." Its bushy tail was commonly used in the East as a fly whisk.

(8) It is an interesting commentary on the life of this period that this Italian left Russia to fight as a private soldier in the Army of the Duke of Alva in the Netherlands, but two years later turned up in London as the first ambassador from Rome to Queen Elizabeth.

(9) The narrative of this voyage of Lancaster is to be found in Hakluyt as " written from the mouth of Edmund Barker, of Ipswich, his lieutenant, in sayd voyage." It is reprinted by Clements R. Markham in " Voyages to the East Indies " (Hakluyt Society, Vol. 56, 1877). It is worth noting that while Lancaster is frequently referred to as a pirate in modern histories his depredations were solely directed against Portuguese ships or Portuguese goods. Barker twice refers to his letting ships go when it was found they were " laden with marchants' goods of Pegu onely."

(10) Sir Thomas Smith, or Smythe, was the first governor of the East India Company, as the Company of Merchants Trading in the East Indies was soon called, and with one break served in this capacity until 1621. He was also interested in the Muscovy Company and in 1604 went as ambassador to Russia. In 1609 he obtained the charter for the Virginia Company and thereafter, until 1620, acted as its secretary. No Englishman of his day was more intimately concerned with the overseas expansion of his country's trade.

(11) For some mysterious reason Lancaster's discovery of the value of lemon juice as a preventive for the " calamity of sailors " was completely ignored. It was not until the voyages of Cook almost two hundred years later that the lesson which might have been learned from Lancaster's experience was really taken to heart. Sir William Osler, in " The Principles and Practice of Medicine," states that it was in 1795 that Sir Gilbert Blake first introduced lime juice into the navy.

(12) It should be remembered that while the King of Achin had had dealings with only the Portuguese, news of the union of Portugal and Spain in 1580 and of England's war against the combined kingdoms had been carried to the East by the Dutch.

(13) On his famous voyage around the world Drake had signed a commercial agreement with the Sultan of Ternate, in the Spice Islands. It had, however, no practical results.

(14) At a later date a Dutch sea captain died from the ill effects of sitting in the water at one of these banquets and drinking too much.

(15) Adams' letters have been printed many times since the discovery of manuscript copies, varying slightly from the texts in Purchas, in the archives of the East India Company. Thomas Rundall, in his " Memorials of the Empire of Japon," printed in 1850 for the Hakluyt Society (Vol. 8), also gives additional letters. More recently Adams' log has been unearthed by C. J. Purnell (Transactions of the Japan Society, Vol. 13, 1914–15).

(16) While the " Hope " must have sunk with all hands the fate of the three other vessels with which Adams' ship had lost touch was less disastrous. The " Faith " and the " Fidelity," unable to make their way about Cape Horn, returned to Europe and reached Holland on January 22, 1600. The " Good News " was captured by the Spanish.

(17) " Japan : An Attempt at Interpretation," by Lafcadio Hearn (New York, 1924).

(18) In the book of Lafcadio Hearn noted above this writer upon Japan states in this connection : " Viewed from another standpoint than that of religious bias, and simply judged by its results, the Jesuit effort to Christianize Japan must be regarded as a crime against humanity, a labour of devastation, a calamity comparable only—by reason of the misery and destruction which it wrought—to an earthquake, a tidal-wave, a volcanic eruption."

(19) This legend has been dramatized by a modern Japanese playright.

(20) As " Hamlet " was not printed until 1603 or 1604 this note in Keeling's diary has a special literary interest as marking one of the first recorded performances of the play. See the appendix of Rundall's " Narrative of Voyages towards the North-West " and the introduction of Markham's " Voyages to the East Indies."

(21) William Hawkins was a nephew of Sir John Hawkins of Armada fame.

(22) Henry Middleton, a brother of John Middleton who had been Lancaster's second-in-command, had also sailed on the East India Company's first voyage. He was in charge of its second venture and went as far east as the Moluccas. The voyage which he commanded at this time was the Company's sixth. A third brother of this family so noted in the exploration of the East was David Middleton. He sailed in 1604 under Henry and subsequently went out in command of the third voyage.

(23) This remarkable diary to which we are indebted for our account of Roe's stay in India appeared in part in Purchas and also in other collections. But it has since been edited from the original

manuscript, together with letters, by Sir William Foster. The
original edition for the Hakluyt Society has now been re-issued
in new and revised form by the Oxford University Press : " The
Embassy of Sir Thomas Roe to India," (London, 1926).

(24) " Memoirs of Emperor Jahangir (Tuzuk-i-Jahangiri)."
Translated by A. Rogers and edited by H. Beveridge. Two
Volumes. (London, 1909 and 1914).

(25) This may seem unusual for such an early period until we
remember that one of Roe's friends and patrons at Court had been
Sir Walter Raleigh !

(26) Coryat expected to remain with Roe until the latter's
return, but his health became so weak that he left for Surat, hoping
to get a passage either to Persia or to England. But there the
hospitality of the English factors, who plied him with sack, was too
much for him and " he overtook death in the month of December,
1617."

(27) This was Anthony à Wood, quoted in Foster's introduction
to " The Embassy of Sir Thomas Roe to India."

SOURCES

Asher, G. M.   Henry Hudson the Navigator.   Hakluyt Society, Vol. 27.   London, 1860.

Barrow, Sir John.   Chronological History of Voyages into the Arctic Regions.   London, 1818.

Beazley, C. Raymond.   John and Sebastian Cabot.   London, 1898.

Brinkley, Captain F.   Japan: Its History, Arts and Literature.   Boston and Tokyo, 1902.

Bruce, John.   Annals of the East India Company.   3 Volumes.   London, 1810.

Calendar of State Papers, East Indies, 1513–1616.   Edited by W. Noel Sainsbury.   London, 1862.

Cawston, George, and Keane, A. H.   The Early Chartered Companies.   London, 1896.

Cocks, Richard, Diary of.   Edited by Sir Edwarde Maude Thompson.   Hakluyt Society, Vols. 66 and 67.   London, 1883.

Cunningham, William.   The Growth of English Industry and Commerce in Modern Times.   Cambridge, 1892.

Danvers, F. C.   "The English Connection with Sumatra."   Asiatic Quarterly Review, Vol. 1, 1886.

Davis, John, Voyages and Works.   Hakluyt Society, Vol. 59.   London, 1880.

Dawn of British Trade to the East Indies.   Edited by Henry Stevens.   London, 1886.

Dictionary of National Biography.   Edited by Leslie Stephen.   London, 1885.

Diosy, Arthur.   Biographical Sketch of William Adams.   Transactions of the Japan Society, Vol. 6.   London, 1901–4.

Early Travels in India, 1583–1619.   Edited by William Foster.   London, 1921.

Early Voyages and Travels to Russia and Persia by Anthony Jenkinson and other Englishmen.   Edited by E. Delmar Morgan and C. H. Coote.   Hakluyt Society, Vols. 72 and 73.   London, 1886.

Eden, Richard.   The History of Travayle.   London, 1577.

First Letter Book of the East India Company, 1600–1619. Edited by Sir George Birdwood and William Foster. London, 1893.

Foster, Sir William. The Embassy of Sir Thomas Roe to India, 1615–19. London, 1926.

Hakluyt, Richard. The Principal Navigations, Voyages, Travels and Discoveries of the English Nation. London, 1600, and Hakluyt Society Extra Series (12 volumes), Glasgow, 1903.

Hamel, Dr. J. England and Russia. Translated by J. S. Leigh. London, 1854.

Hildreth, Richard. Japan As it Was and Is. New York, 1853.

Hunter, Sir William W. A History of British India. 2 Volumes. London, 1899.

Kaempffer, Engelbert. The History of Japan. Translated by J. G. Schenchzer. 2 Vols. London, 1827.

Lancaster, Sir James, Voyages to the East Indies, Edited by Clements R. Markham. Hakluyt Society, Vol. 56. London 1877.

Letters Received by the East India Company from its Servants in the East. Edited by F. C. Danvers and William Foster. London, 1896–1902.

Lockhart, R. H. Bruce. The First Englishman in Russia. The Fortnightly Review, No. 738. London, 1928.

Lubimenko, Inna. The Correspondence of Queen Elizabeth with the Russian Czars. American Historical Review, April, 1914.

Lucas, Sir C. P. The Beginnings of English Overseas Enterprise. Oxford, 1917.

Malcolm, Sir John. The History of Persia. London, 1815.

Marsden, William. The History of Sumatra. London, 1784.

Memoirs of Emperor Jahangir (Tuzuk-i-Jahangiri). Translated by A. Rogers and edited by H. Beveridge. 2 Vols. London 1909 and 1914.

Middleton, Sir Henry. Voyage to Bantam and the Maluco Islands. Hakluyt Society, Volume 29. London 1855.

Murdock, James and Yamagada, Isok. History of Japan during the century of Early Foreign Intercourse (1542–1651.) Kobe, 1903.

Pelsaert, Francisco, The Remonstrantie of (Jahangir's India). Translated by W. H. Moreland and P. Geyl. Cambridge, 1925.

Purchas, Samuel. Hakluytus Posthumus or Purchas His Pilgrimes.

London, 1625, and Hakluyt Society Extra Series (20 Vols.) Glasgow, 1907.

Purnell, C. J. The Log Book of William Adams. Transactions of the Japan Society, Vol. 13. London, 1914-5.

Rawlinson, H. G. British Beginnings in Western India, 1579–1657. Oxford, 1920.

Reresdale, the Rt. Hon. Lord. 300 Years Ago. Transactions of the Japan Society, Vol. 8. London, 1907-09.

Riess, Dr. Ludwig. History of the English Factory at Hirado. Transactions of the Asiatic Society (Japan), Vol. 26. Tokyo, 1898.

Rundall, Thomas. Memorials of the Empire of Japan. Hakluyt Society, Vol. 8. London, 1850.

Rundall, Thomas. Narratives of Voyages towards the North-West in Search of a Passage to Cathay and India. Hakluyt Society, Vol. 5. London, 1849.

Sakamoto, Kiyoshi. The Romance of Will Adams. The Far East (Tokyo). January 18, 1919.

Satow, Sir Ernest M. The Voyage of Captain John Saris. Hakluyt Society, 2nd Series, Vol. 5. London, 1900.

Studies in the History of English Commerce in the Tudor Period. University of Pennsylvania, 1912.

Terry, Rev. Edward. A Voyage to East India. London, 1655.

Veer, Gerrit de. A True Description of three Voyages by the North-east towards Cathay and China. Edited by Charles T. Beke. Hakluyt Society, Vol. 13. London, 1853.

Waliszewski, K. Ivan the Terrible. London, 1904.

Williamson, James A. Maritime Enterprise—1485-1558. Oxford 1913.

Williamson, James A. A Short History of British Expansion. London, 1922.

Willson, Beckles. Ledger and Sword. London, 1903.

Wright, Arnold. Early English Adventurers in the East. London, 1917.

NOTE.—Selections from the original accounts of the voyages of Chancellor, Jenkinson, Lancaster, Adams and Roe are also to be found in innumerable collections of voyages and travels published from the seventeenth century to the twentieth, and in French and German as well as in English.

INDEX

ABDULLAH KHAN, King of Bokhara, 48–51
Abdullah Khan, King of Shirvan, 56–57, 61
Achin, *see* Chapter IX, 104, 135
Adams, Clement, *quoted*, 5–6, 10, 14, 20, 27; 187 n.
Adams, Thomas, 117
Adams, William, early life, 113–114; voyage to Japan, 114–120; goes to Japanese Court, 121–127; relations with Iyeyasu, 127–132; life in Japan, 132–134; aids English, 135–143; plans voyage to north-east, 144–145; final days and death, 146–149; mentioned, 153, 157, 175
Agra, 155, 156, 158, 183
Ahmadabad, 180, 182
Ajmere, 165, 166, 174, 176, 180
Akbar, 153, 154, 155, 168
Ala-uddin Shah, King of Achin, 94–98, 99, 101, 102, 103
Annobon, island of, 115
Arundel, Earl of, 28
"Ascension," the, 87, 89
Astrakhan, 41, 52, 56, 62, 63
"Ayde," the, 64
Ayuthia, 146

BAFFIN, William, 109
Balkh, 51
Bantam, 104, 105, 106, 135
Bengal, 100, 154
Best, Thomas, 155, 156
Bodenham, Roger, 2
Bokhara, 47–49, 50, 51, 56, 63

"Bona Confidentia," the, 2, 3, 13, 14, 23, 24, 34
"Bona Esperanza," the, 2, 3, 13, 15, 23, 24, 34
Buckland, John, 2
Bungo, 120, 121, 122, 128
Burhanpur, 166
Burroughs, Stephen, 2, 32, 33

CABOT, John, 6, 36
Cabot, Sebastian, 9, 10, 11, 13, 15, 28, 40, 106
Cape Corrientes, 81
Cape Gonsalves, 115
Cape Horn, 79, 115, 116, 144
Cape of Good Hope, 6, 77, 79, 81, 82, 89, 106, 115, 144, 153, 162
Caspian Sea, 41, 42, 48, 50, 56, 62, 77
Cathay Company, 78
Cathay, goal of north-east voyages, 1, 5–9, 12, 15, 16, 24, 26, 39, 50–51, 63–64, 77–79, 83; mentioned, 3, 47, 53, 80, 114, 144, 154
Cave, Sir Thomas, 161
Cavendish, Thomas, 1, 77, 79, 80
Cecil, Sir William, 28, 65
Chancellor, Richard, early life, 2; first voyage, 2, 5, 9–10, 13–23; second voyage, 26–36 *passim*; at Russian Court, 19–21, 29–30; trade agreements with Ivan, 22–23, 30–32; death, 35; mentioned, 39, 40, 66, 77, 80, 81, 106, 144, 157
"Charity," the, 114, 117–121 *passim*, 127, 128, 148

Charles I, 184
Charlevoix, Catholic historian, 130
China, 7, 105, 130, 165 ; see Cathay
Cipangu, 3, 6, 114, 118
" Clove," the, 135, 136, 137, 142, 143
Cochin China, 130, 145
Cocks, Richard, 142, 143, 148
Columbus, 3, 6, 36
Comoro Island, 162
Coryat, Thomas, 176–177, 190 n.
Cumberland, Earl of, 84, 87

Davis, John, 1, 77, 79, 87, 91, 95, 114
Derbend, 56
Deshima, 149
Diaz, Bartholomew, 6, 36
Diggins, Nicholas, 113, 131
Downtown, Nicholas, 156–157
" Dragon," the, 137 ; see " Red
     Dragon," the
Drake, Sir Francis, 1, 77, 79, 80, 81,
     114, 115, 188 n.
Dvina, River, 16, 29, 33, 41

East India Company, formation of,
     84, 188 n. ; and Lancaster,
     86–88, 92, 98, 106–109 ; and
     Adams, 113, 128, 135, 137,
     142–147 ; early trade with
     India, 154–155, 163 ; and
     Roe, 158–159, 161, 170, 176–
     178, 183, 185 ; mentioned,
     10, 77, 83, 114, 153, 189 n.
East Indies, see Indies
Edward VI, 1, 3–4, 5, 9, 17, 20, 22,
     26, 27, 87
" Edward Bonaventure," the (1), 2,
     3, 4, 13, 17, 22–35 passim,
     40, 81
" Edward Bonaventure," the (2) 81,
     82
Edwards, William, 157–158
Elizabeth, and Jenkinson, 54, 55, 58,
     60, 66–72 ; relations with
     Czar Ivan, 66–72 ; promotes
     eastern voyages, 79, 83, 84 ;
     and Lancaster, 87, 93, 95–98,

101, 103, 105, 106 ; relations
     with King of Achin, 93, 95–
     98, 101, 103 ; death, 109 ;
     mentioned, 1, 8, 85, 113, 114,
     123, 125, 126, 144, 154, 157,
     160
Elizabeth, Princess, 160

" Faith," the, 114, 189 n.
Fenton, Edward, 77, 79
" Fidelity," the, 114, 189 n.
Fitch, Ralph, 154
Franciscans, 129
Frobisher, Martin, 1, 77–78
Frothingham, Christopher, 18

Genghis Khan, 44, 47
Georgia, 62
Gilbert, Sir Humphrey, 8
Gillingham, 113, 134
Goa, 153, 154
" Golden Hind," the, 79
" Good News," the, 114, 189 n.
Gray, Richard, 29
Greenwich, 3, 4, 23
Gresham, Sir John, 28
Gresham, Sir Thomas, 28
Grey, Lady Jane, 26, 27
" Guest," the, 88

Hadjim Khan, 45
Hakluyt, Richard, 7, 35, 73, 78
Hall, Rev. John, 176, 185
Hamlet, 137, 189 n.
Harwich, 4, 13
Hawkins, Sir John, 189 n.
Hawkins, William, 154–155, 156,
     189 n.
Hearn, Lafcadio, 124, 134
" Hector," the, 87, 89, 104, 107, 108
Hemi-Mura, 132, 133, 142, 148
Henry VIII, 7
Henry, Prince, 160
Hideyoshi, 123
Hirado, 135, 137, 141–147 passim
Hitetada, 146, 147, 149

Holland, 83, 92, 104, 114, 118, 120, 128
"Hope," the, 114, 117, 119, 189 n.
Houtman, Cornelius, 83, 87, 114
Howard, Lord, 28, 81
Hudson, Henry, 8

INDIA, see Chapters XIV, XV, XVI
Indian Ocean, 81, 82, 83, 85, 86, 90
Indies, 5, 7, 54, 77, 80, 83, 85, 87, 88, 91, 104, 109, 115, 118, 154
Ivan, Czar of Russia, power of, 16, 18–19; and Chancellor, 20–22, 28–32; and Jenkinson, 41, 53, 55–56, 62, 64–72; relations with Elizabeth, 66–72; mentioned, 125, 155, 157
Iyeyasu, Shogun of Japan, position of, 122, 123–125; and Adams, 125–134, 142, 144; and later English traders, 139, 141, 143; death, 146; mentioned, 155, 157, 170

JACKMAN, Charles, 8, 77, 78
Jahangir, the Great Mogul, early attitude toward English, 155, 157, 158; and Roe, 161, 165–173, 177–183, 185; at court, 169–173; on the march, 180–182
James I, 109, 135, 139, 141, 153, 159, 160, 165, 167, 183, 184, 185
Japan, see Chapters XI, XII, XIII
Java, 104
Jenkinson, Anthony, early life, 39–40; journey to Bokhara, 40–53; journey to Persia, 54–62; and North-East Passage, 8, 63–64; in Russia, 64–67, 70–72; and Ivan, 41, 53, 55–56, 62, 64–72; death, 73; mentioned, 77, 80, 113, 114, 125, 144, 145, 157
Jesuits, in Japan, 121, 122, 126, 129, 130, 131, 133, 136; in India, 154, 159

KAMAKURA, 141
Kashgar, 50
Kath, 45
Kazan, 19
Kazvin, 57–63 passim
Keeling, William, 137, 161, 189 n.
Khiva, 45
Kholmogory, 31, 33, 41
Khurram, Prince, 158, 178, 182 see Shah Jehan
Killingworth, George, 29, 30
Kyoto, 139, 141
Kyp, Cornelis, 144
Kyushu, 120

LANCASTER, James, early life, 80; first voyage to East, 81–83; and East India Company, 77, 85–88; voyage to Achin, 89–103; in Java, 104–106; return to England, 106–108; death, 109; mentioned, 114, 135, 153, 157, 162
Lane, Henry, 53
Lapland, 23, 24
Leedes, William, 154
Leicester, Earl of, 64
"Lion," the, 161

"MADRE DE DEOS," the, 80
Magellan, Ferdinand, 77, 115
Mahu, Jacques, 114
Malacca, 81, 85, 92, 100
"Malice Scourge," the, see "Red Dragon," the
Mandu, 180, 182
Mary, Queen, 26, 27, 34, 40
Mary, Queen of Scots, 64
Médici, Catherine de, 64
Mercator, Gerardus, 8
Michelborne, Sir Edward, 84
Middleton, David, 189 n.
Middleton, Henry, 155, 189 n.
Middleton, John, 87, 189 n.
Mildenhall, 154
Moluccas, 7, 91, 106
Mona, island of, 82

Moscow, 16, 17–18, 21, 29, 31, 32, 33, 40, 41; 53–56, 62–70, *passim*
Muscovy, *see* Russia
Muscovy Company, 27–28, 40, 54, 64, 65, 66, 69, 71, 72

NAGASAKI, 147, 149
Napea, Osep, 34, 35, 40, 55
Nenoksa, 16, 17
Newbery, John, 154
Nobunaga, 123
North Cape, 13, 23, 25, 29, 50
North-East Passage, 6–9, 32, 63–64, 78–79, 144–145
North-West Passage, 9, 77–78
Norway, 13
Novaya Zemlya, 24, 32
Novgorod, 19, 21, 31, 41
Nur Mahal, 171, 178, 181

OSAKA, 122, 123, 124, 140

PAGES, Catholic historian, 130
Parwiz, Prince, 166
Patagonia, 116
Penang, 81, 85
Pereslavl, 71
Pernambuco, 85, 86
Perry, Commodore, 124, 132
Persia, 50, 51, 56–63 *passim*
Pet, Arthur, 8, 77, 78
Peter the Great, 32, 67
Philip II of Spain, 26, 27, 34, 40, 121
" Philip and Mary," the, 28, 29, 32, 33, 34
Poland, 32, 65, 67
Polo, Marco, 1, 50, 91, 119
Portugal, 6, 7, 11, 77, 79, 80, 82, 83, 91, 99, 114, 153, 156
" Primrose," the, 40
Purchas His Pilgrimes, 90, 115

RALEIGH, Sir Walter, 160, 190 n.
Randolph, Thomas, 67–68
Ratcliffe, 1
Raymond, George, 80, 81

" Red Dragon," the, 87, 89, 104, 107, 108, 137
" Richard Duffield," the, 114
Roe, Sir Thomas, early life and appointment by East India Company, 153, 159–161; journey to Mogul Court, 162–166; and Jahangir, 166–173; life at Ajmere, 174–180; on the march with Jahangir, 180–183; negotiations for treaty, 177–179, 182–183; return and death, 183–185
Romanoff, Nikita, 31
Russia, *see* Chapters III, IV, 39, 40, 53; Chapter VII, 77, 113
Ryukyu Islands, 145

SAINT HELENA, 108
Samarkand, 47, 48, 51, 63
San Domingo, 82
" San Felipe," the, 80
Santa Maria, island of, 117
Saris, Captain John, 135, 136, 138–143, 147
Savin, Andrew, 69
" Sea Adventure," the, 145, 146, 148
Senjen, island of, 13
" Serchthrift," the, 32–33
Shabran, 56
Shah Jehan, 158, 182, 183; *see* Prince Khurram
Shemakha, 56, 58
Shirvan, 56, 61
Siam, 100, 130, 145, 146, 154
Sidney, Henry, 2, 10
Sidney, Sir Philip, 2
Smythe, Sir Thomas, 145, 158, 188 n.
Sokotra, 162
Southampton, Earl of, 160
Spain, 6, 7, 9, 11, 77, 79, 84, 93
Spanish Armada, 79, 114
Spice Islands, 77, 80, 82, 85, 86, 91, 113, 114
Spitzbergen, 144
Stevens, Thomas, 153–154
Story, James, 154

Sumatra, *see* Chapter IX
Surat, 154-155, 156, 158, 162-166
    passim, 177, 182, 183, 184
Surunga, 140, 141
" Susan," the, 87, 89
" Swallow," the, 55

TABLE BAY, 90
Tahmasp, Shah of Persia, 58-61
Tashkend, 50
Terry, Edward, 185, 186
Texel, island of, 114, 119, 148
Thorne, Robert, 7, 8, 15, 63, 187 n.
Timur, 47
Tokkaido, the, 139-140
Trondhjem, 34
Turberville, George, 18
Turkey, 58, 59, 62

URAGA, 129, 132
Urgendj, 45, 51

VARDO, 13, 14, 16, 24, 29
Vasco da Gama, 6, 36
Volga, River, 41, 43, 56
Vologda, 29, 31, 34, 41

WEST INDIES, 82
Willoughby, Sir Hugh, sails for
    Cathay, 2, 5, 9 ; fate of, 23-
    25 ; mentioned, 31, 39, 106
Winchester, Marquis of, 27
Wood, Benjamin, 77, 83

YEDO, 124, 132, 139, 140, 141, 146

ZULFAKER KHAN, 158, 164-165

GLASSBORO STATE COLLEGE